Commodity Trading
A Beginner's Guide

by
Jay and Julie Hawk

First edition.

Copyright © 2017 Jay and Julie Hawk

www.thefxperts.com

All rights reserved. This book or any portion thereof
may not be reproduced or used in any manner whatsoever
without the express written permission of the authors
except for the use of brief quotations in a book review.

ISBN-13: 978-1981776320
ISBN-10: 198177632X

DEDICATION

This book is dedicated to our dear family who loved us, believed in us and encouraged us to excel in our chosen professions

JAY AND JULIE HAWK

TABLE OF CONTENTS

	Dedication	iii
	Table of Contents	v
	Acknowledgements	vii
	Foreword	ix
1	Commodity Trading Basics	Pg #1
2	The Commodity Market	Pg #19
3	Getting Started Trading Commodities	Pg #37
4	Popular Commodities to Trade	Pg #61
5	Commodity Trading Strategies	Pg #85
6	Commodity Price Analysis	Pg #101
7	Money and Risk Management for Commodity Traders	Pg #131
8	Commodity Trader Psychology	Pg #145
9	Commodity Trading as a Business	Pg #161
10	Parting Advice for Commodity Traders	Pg #171
11	Recommended Further Reading	Pg #181
	About the Authors	Pg #185
	Glossary	Pg #189
	Index	Pg #203

ACKNOWLEDGMENTS

This book is the product of many years of personal experience and research obtained by working professionally in the financial markets, trading for our own accounts, and writing about trading as freelancers. We want to thank those who brought us up, those who taught us how to trade, and those who paid us to write for them.

FOREWORD

As long term experts in the field of financial markets and derivatives trading, one of the most exciting things we have had the opportunity to witness personally in our careers was the electronification of the major commodity markets and the advent of online CFD trading for retail speculators. That meant individuals no longer had to be a high-net worth individual, producer, corporation or a market professional to buy and sell commodities, and they could far more efficiently trade commodities for profit.

Once that evolution happened, almost anyone could then open up a margin trading account with an online Contract for Difference or CFD broker and trade commodity CFDs speculatively on margin, even if they only had a small stake to put at risk. All they needed was a reasonably modern computer connected to the Internet that they could run an electronic trading platform on.

With relatively sophisticated trading software like MetaTrader available freely as downloadable software, that just made the commodity market even more accessible to virtually any person who wanted to get involved. This remarkable phenomenon notably changed the formerly structured and highly regulated world of commodity trading dramatically. Now the general public wanted to try their hands at speculating on commodity price movements too!

Over the years since that major commodity market evolution occurred, we have been on the forefront of educating the increasingly savvy public about how to trade commodities and other financial markets profitably. Even for many experienced traders, operating successfully in the commodity market can be a challenge due to the inherent volatility of many commodity prices. Inexperienced traders were further hampered by their lack of knowledge about how to trade and what fundamental factors move prices in the commodity market.

The harsh reality remains that without a solid foundation, most buildings do not last very long, and the same holds true for commodity traders. Without a solid educational foundation and a good working understanding of how the commodity market operates and how to make money consistently when trading, the margin accounts of most would-be commodity operators are quickly depleted.

Knowing this all too well, we aimed to use our insider expertise obtained working as professional traders to help such retail commodity traders by writing widely on the subject for numerous Internet websites so that they could freely access this insider information. Working for over a decade as freelance writers, we have at this point contributed thousands articles to this information pool, as well as online courses, e-books and reports. We even ghostwrote published books on the subject of financial markets that were attributed to other writers.

With this book, we offer the third in a series of planned books on the financial markets to share our knowledge and expertise in trading the commodity market with the public in a different format. Our intention in publishing a book under our own names is to take a higher-profile role in educating prospective traders realistically about what is involved in trading commodities profitably and to complement the background of more experienced traders with professional methods and techniques that they may not yet be familiar with. Successful commodity trading is not exactly easy, but it does not have to be overly difficult either, especially with access to the proper tools and education.

This beginner's guide to commodity trading is designed to give traders and prospective traders a solid foundation to build upon as they operate in the commodity market. We intend to do this by sharing our insider knowledge about the different established trading methods and market analysis tools. We also share what worked for us as we took the benefit of our differing professional backgrounds and applied our knowledge to the task of trading commodity CFDs in our own personal accounts using MetaTrader4 and the easy commodity market access offered by online CFD brokers.

In addition to covering the basics about the commodity markets that any commodity trader needs to know, this book contains detailed information about opening an online trading account and getting familiar with using an electronic trading platform. It also covers how to get started trading commodities using some basic trading strategies and money management techniques that can be applied immediately in your trading business.

The chapter on commodity price analysis introduces the trader to the essential tools of technical analysis as it pertains to commodities, which can be extremely useful in determining entry and exit points for trades. We also introduce the other major analysis method of fundamental analysis, since such factors can often move the market regardless of a commodity's technical condition and need to be a part of any trader's understanding of the commodity market.

Further on the book, our chapter on money management explains optimal ways of managing risk for the size of your trading account and gives the trader prudent position sizing and other money management techniques to start applying immediately. What many novice traders fail to realize is that by using an intelligent method of money management, a commodity trader can be successful even if they are wrong more than half of the time on the direction of the market.

We think that one of the most important segments of this book is the trader psychology chapter since understanding your psychological makeup and how to manage your emotions when trading is a key element to success. Knowing how you react to different market situations and cultivating the optimal trading mindset can really make the difference between turning a profit or a loss in the commodity market. This section of the book illustrates the various types of traders and explains how they typically react to different market situations and emotional experiences.

In the next chapter of this book, we put together the knowledge from previous chapters to help the reader make commodity trading a viable business proposition for them and any potential investors they might wish to attract. Our chapter on commodity trading as a business distills the methods previously illustrated to help you run a successful commodity trading business, just as we have run our trading business. Using appropriate discretion, a comprehensive and easy to follow trading plan, and sound money management techniques, we think that any person of reasonable intelligence can become a successful commodity trader.

We then conclude the book by offering some helpful tips that we learned when we started to trade that contributed to our success, and that we think any trader would probably benefit from internalizing. We also provide a glossary of terms you can refer to as you start to decipher the often colorful jargon that professional commodity traders use to communicate with each other; some recommended additional reading to further your trading education; and a bit of information about our professional backgrounds to establish our authority to educate on this subject.

While the age-old trading goal of "buying low and selling high" continues to be the key when pursuing a profit in any market, having some decent insider knowledge under your belt can help you better discern what levels are high and what levels are low. This does not mean that traders need to overcomplicate their trading decisions; especially since many of the most successful commodity trading plans and techniques can be extremely simple and are often the most profitable since they are the easiest to apply quickly in a fast moving market.

Overall, we think this third book on trading in our financial series makes an excellent introduction to what can appear to be a complicated subject. In writing it, we intended for this introductory book to inspire and educate both novice and seasoned traders alike, and we wish our readers great success in their commodity trading careers and hope they enjoy them as much as we have ours.

Jay and Julie Hawk
www.thefxperts.com
Sonora, Mexico, December, 2017

CHAPTER 1: COMMODITY TRADING BASICS

What is a commodity exactly? Well, a commodity is a basic physical good used in commerce that is employed as an input when producing other goods or services. Commodities are generally interchangeable with others of the same type, and while a given commodity may differ slightly in quality, it is basically the same across its various producers. Soft commodities like coffee are those that come from agriculture, while hard commodities like gold are mined.

Furthermore, any introduction to commodity trading needs to clarify that a commodity purchase transaction involves the exchange of currency for a certain amount of a commodity, while a commodity sale transaction involves the exchange of an amount of a commodity for currency. The price at which this transaction or trade takes place is determined by market factors, such as the supply and demand for the commodity and the relative value of the currency its price is denominated in.

Commodities typically trade on exchanges or organized marketplaces where transactions are subject to local regulations. Many of these commodity exchanges exist in countries around the world and list the prices of commodities important to local producers using derivatives like futures and options contracts and Contracts for Difference or CFDs. An active Over the Counter or OTC market for commodity forwards and options also exists that mainly caters to producers looking to hedge their commodity risks.

As of 2016, the size of the global commodities derivatives market is estimated at around $750 billion. This impressive size and recent growth in market turnover has accompanied increased investment in commodity indexes, as well as the growth of commodity hedge funds that speculate in commodities. Additional market growth has come from mutual funds that specialize in natural resources investment.

What are Commodities?

In general, commodities are physical products such as foods, textiles, metals, energy products, construction materials, plastics and any other products used for human or animal consumption or to produce other products with.

Also traded on some commodities exchanges are financial products, such as currencies and debt securities, as well as indexes on stocks, metals and other indexes. The rest of this section covers what commodities are, how commodities affect people in their daily lives and how commodities are traded.

Agricultural and Food Commodities

Commodities touch practically every human in the world in one way or another. Unless a person is living in complete isolation in a self-contained and completely independent community where all goods are produced and provided for, commodities will have some effect.

As an example, a good proportion of the human population is involved in the production of food. The food must be grown or raised, harvested or slaughtered and finally processed and packaged for final human consumption.

From the fields to the dinner table, the commodities which include grains, meats and vegetables have passed through the hands of the producer, distributor and finally the merchant before arriving at your home, and employing thousands of people in the process in some cases.

Other commodities such as coffee or sugar for example are often produced and refined or roasted in other countries employing even more people in the shipping and handling of the product.

By the time an agricultural or food commodity reaches the end-consumer it may have travelled thousands of miles, employed thousands of people in its production and will feed countless people when it is finally distributed and consumed.

Energy Commodities

Another way commodities affect everyone is energy. Oil and gasoline are two of the most important energy commodities with their prices affecting billions of people all over the world. The price of oil affects transportation costs for all goods and directly impacts the world economy.

In addition to their uses in transportation, petroleum and its by-products are used in the production of a variety of other goods including plastics such as polyvinyl chloride and polypropylene used in the manufacture of thousands of plastic items.

Precious and Minor Metals

Gold and silver have been the traditional wealth storage vehicles having been used for thousands of years in the making of coins and jewelry. These commodities are actively traded and provide a hedge for inflation. In addition to the precious metals, which also include platinum and palladium, a number of "minor metals" which include copper, tin, steel and molybdenum are extremely important in industry and also directly affect prices on many items.

Basically, commodities impact everyone in one way or another. Even the clothes you wear are priced according to prices set on cotton or on petroleum if they are made of synthetic fabric.

Commodities are traded around the world in commodities exchanges, electronic trading platforms and telephone networks. Trading in commodities is not an exclusive endeavor and anyone with a relatively small amount of money has the possibility of trading commodities, however it is highly recommended to research the commodity market thoroughly before trading, the commodities market can be extremely risky depending on which commodity you choose to trade.

A Brief History of Commodity Trading

Commodity trading as practiced today has its origins in China where evidence of futures contracts for rice date back more than six thousand years. Trading futures on commodities were the direct result of the difficulty in maintaining a store of seasonal products such as agricultural crops for the entire year.

More recent evidence dates to 17th century Japan where merchants stored rice in warehouses for future consumption. Warehouse owners would sell receipts called "rice tickets" against the stored rice in order to raise cash.

These rice tickets eventually became accepted as a type of commercial currency which later became standardized. A market for standardized rice tickets was then established with set rules which later would become the basis for modern American futures trading.

Modern Commodity Trading

Modern commodity trading has its roots in the Midwestern farmlands of the United States around the 1840s or thereabouts. The McCormick reaper, a machine used in harvesting grain had just been invented which resulted in a much higher amount of wheat harvested.

Chicago was the main hub for dealers to buy grain for shipment to the East coast and in 1848 a central location or "exchange" was opened for farmers and dealers to exchange cash for grain at a "spot" price for immediate delivery, the exchange became the Chicago Board of Trade.

Futures contracts evolved as farmers and dealers contracted for future grain deliveries eventually formalizing and standardizing futures contracts.

Where Commodities Trade

Commodities exchanges now thrive all over the world; however, certain exchanges specialize in certain types of commodity products. In the United States for example, the Chicago Board of Trade was established in 1848 and pioneered futures trading. It continues to be the foremost trading arena for soybeans, oats, wheat and corn.

The Chicago Mercantile Exchange is the principle exchange for livestock and dairy products and recently merged with both the Chicago Board of Trade and with the New York Mercantile Exchange that specializes in energy commodities. These mergers created the largest commodities futures exchange in the world that is now called the CME Group.

In addition to the U.S. commodities exchanges, other commodities exchanges, such as the London Metals Exchange, serve as a principle market for non-ferrous metals as well as precious metals and other important metal products.

India and China also have commodities exchanges that focus on products of local importance. India's three principle exchanges specialize in spices, minor metals and plastics, while China's two primary exchanges specialize in metals, minor metals, plastics and agricultural commodities.

Commodities have an important role in world economics and literally make the world go round. Everything from the food on your table to the gas in your car to the clothes you wear is commodities-related and has been traded in one way or another before being consumed.

Commodities trading both for the general public as well as for commercial and financial institutions normally consist of futures, or contracts for future delivery of the commodity, which are generally traded on any of a number of commodity exchanges throughout the world.

Commodities Exchanges

Commodities actively trade on centralized commodity exchanges, where standardized commodity contracts for future delivery trade. These contracts, known as "futures contracts" typically obligate the seller to deliver a specified quantity of a commodity to the buyer of the contract at a pre-determined future date for a particular price.

Futures contracts are standardized. This means that the commodity for which the contract is written meets certain standards of quality and is in a particular quantity, thereby ensuring the buyer of the contract receives a quality product in an expected amount according to the standards set forth by the exchange.

Major Global Commodities Exchanges

The major commodities exchanges in the world where the majority of physical commodity futures contracts trade include:

- **The Chicago Mercantile Exchange or CME Group** – recently merged with the Chicago Board of Trade CBOT and the New York Mercantile Exchange or NYMEX which includes the COMEX. The CME Group trades over 90 percent of all exchange-traded futures in the United States.

- **The London Metals Exchange** – the largest precious and base metals exchange in the world.

- **The Multi-Commodity Exchange or MCX and the National Multi-Commodity and Derivatives Exchange or NCDEX** – both from India are the world's largest exchanges for spices and other exotic commodities.

- **The Dalian Commodities Exchange** – the largest commodities exchange in China where commodities such as plastics, oilseed and steel are traded.

How Commodities Trade

As discussed in the previous section, commodities are generally traded on exchanges in the form of futures contracts, futures contracts are contracts for delivery of a certain quantity of a commodity at a specific place within a certain period of time.

These contracts are standardized with minimum specifications of quality and delivery of the commodity and are generally offset with cash. It is estimated that only 2% of total commodity futures contracts traded result in the delivery of the commodity.

Spot Market

In commodities, securities and foreign exchange market terminology, the spot market, also known as the cash and physical market, generally refers to an "over-the-counter" or OTC market in which commodities, securities or currencies are bought and sold for "immediate" delivery.

"Over-the-counter" refers to a market which is not a centralized securities or commodities exchange, and transactions typically take place over a telephone network or in a central location such as a wholesale market where deliveries can be made shortly after purchase.

"Immediate" delivery in the spot market is typically seven business days for commodities and securities, while it is two business days for most currency pairs, other than USD/CAD which is one. Nevertheless, some perishable exchange-traded commodities, such as butter and cheese for example, can be traded for same-day delivery.

Commodity Futures and Forward Contracts

Futures contracts consist of standardized contracts traded on major commodities exchanges and can be settled either with delivery of the commodity or offset by buying back the futures contract previously sold, or, by selling a contract previously purchased. An estimated 99% of futures contracts are offset with cash before the delivery date.

A forward contract on the other hand consists of a custom contract entered between a purchaser and seller which does not have a standardized delivery date and generally ends with the commodity or asset being accepted for delivery. Forward contract may or may not be offset financially depending on the contracting parties. Exchange traded futures however, can almost always be offset before the delivery date unless they are for same-day delivery as is the case with "spot-call" contracts.

Futures on commodities have specific economic purposes despite being vehicles for speculation which provides very little economic benefit. The main benefit futures provide is the ability to "hedge," giving the producer of the commodity an assurance to sell the commodity at a specified price in the future and the purchaser of the commodity a set price that is guaranteed regardless of the commodity's price increasing during the period the futures contract is open.

The other economic benefit that futures provide involves indicating the price of the commodity when a cash market for the commodity is unavailable or where the cash market is not sufficiently developed. The future's price will give a clear indication of what a fair spot price for the commodity might be.

Different Types of Commodities

Commodities futures trading encompass a wide variety of material goods from cereal grains to palladium. Commodities fall into several different categories depending on the nature of the commodity's origin.

Many commodities futures and other derivatives are traded on commodities exchanges and on electronic trading platforms. The most popular commodities to trade include:

- **Agricultural commodities** – all commodities which are grown and harvested, these products are further divided into:
    - *Grains*, which include corn, oats, wheat, soybeans, etc.
    - *Softs*, which include coffee, sugar, cocoa and frozen orange juice.
    - *Spices*, such as coriander, cardamom and other spices.

- **Precious Metals** – metals which act as a storage of wealth and the making of jewelry as well as in other industrial uses such as gold, platinum, silver and palladium
- **Livestock** – commodities which are raised and used for human consumption such as live hogs, pork bellies and feeder and live cattle.
- **Dairy Products** – Milk, Dry Milk, Dry Whey
- **Energies** – commodities that are consumed for the production of power, heating and transportation such as petroleum and its by-products, kerosene, propane, heating oil, natural gas, coal, crude oil, diesel and gasoline.
- **Plastics** – commodities such as linear low density polyethylene, polypropylene and polyvinyl chloride
- **Industrial Metals** – these metals are generally used industrially and include steel, copper, tin, molybdenum and nickel

Commodity Speculation

Trading in commodities has grown into a multi-trillion dollar industry with traders all over the world speculating on price movements for a wide range of commodities. While hedging is still a viable strategy for suppliers and dealers, speculators make up the bulk of commodity traders giving liquidity to the markets.

While many people have benefitted substantially from trading in the commodities markets, a word of caution to those new to trading. A large amount of risk may be involved in the trading of commodities whether leveraged or not and many people who begin trading without a good general market education wind up losing all their money invested. It pays to learn as much about commodities and trading before jumping in with both feet.

A Second Income from Trading Commodities?

Fortunately, the ability to execute commodity transactions has never been as readily available to so many people, as it is today. Gone are the days when a normal person had to call their commodity futures broker to find out where the market was trading on a particular commodity or check the commodity closing price listings in a major newspaper.

The 21st century has truly arrived with respect to the various commodity markets, as modern technology and the rise of Contract for

Difference or CFD trading makes them accessible to a wide online audience that grows daily. Thanks to this new opportunity to trade commodities online, many people can also work jobs as they trade commodities in their spare time. Some of the more successful traders have even used their income trading commodities to replace their jobs so they can now enjoy more time at home with their families.

If taking the risks inherent in trading commodities seems right for your particular financial situation, do remember to cultivate the discipline and patience that will keep you in business as a commodity trader over the long term. Reading this book thoroughly will definitely set you on the right track to success as a commodity trader, but having the discipline typically required to trade profitably is entirely up to you.

What are Physical Commodities?

Physical commodities can be defined in general terms as material goods for which a demand exists in the market. Furthermore, physical commodities need to be fungible, meaning that they are uniform in quality no matter where they are produced or by whom.

In finance, a physical commodity refers to the product that is delivered to a contract buyer once a commodity contract on either the spot, forward or futures market is completed.

The rest of this article explains the nature of physical commodities and how they are traded on the spot market and on commodity exchanges.

Examples of physical commodities include:
- Grains such as wheat and soybeans
- Energy products such as petroleum and heating oil
- Livestock such as live hogs and cattle
- Precious metals such as gold and silver.

Physical commodities also include a wide variety of other goods, such as spices, plastics, base metals, coffee, cotton and frozen orange juice.

What Causes Commodity Price Changes?

Many traders new to the commodity market reasonably wonder what causes commodity price changes. As is the case with most markets, the prevailing price for a commodity represents the value at which supply and demand factors find balance. As a result, the simple answer is that when there are more buyers than sellers in the market the market price moves up, and when there are more sellers than buyers it moves down.

Unfortunately, determining why this balance of supply and demand has shifted in the first place can be quite complex and often requires an advanced understanding of the economic and political environment of those producing and requiring each of the commodities involved.

Later chapters will return to this important topic, but some of the key commodity market-moving factors are listed and their effects explained below.

Key Commodity Price Movement Factors

A list of the main fundamental factors that commodity market participants commonly assess when performing fundamental analysis follows:

- **Political Influences** – the commodities produced by countries that have more stable government politics and are at peace tend to have lower and more stable prices than those produced by less politically stable countries or those at war since supply is more consistent. Also, political and legislative changes in a country can affect commodity prices, as can multi-national pricing collusion in the form of cartel creation. Some countries may also intervene in commodity markets to maintain the value of their fiat currencies.

- **Related Commodity Price Changes** – Higher crude oil prices tend to result in rises in the prices of other energy products. While higher gold prices tend to boost the prices of other precious metals like silver, palladium and platinum.

- **Meteorological and Geological Events** – The weather and other geological occurrences that affect the supply of a commodity can notably affect its price. For example, an unseasonal freeze in Florida can dramatically adversely affect the state's orange crop, which in turn will cause orange juice futures to rise in price.

- **Supply and Demand Effects** – Large speculative or production-driven capital flows into one commodity at the expense of another can boost the price of the commodity in greater demand. Such effects can arise from large shifts in production inputs by major corporations or when a big hedge fund manager's commodity investment portfolio shifts out of one commodity and into another. In addition, production supply factors can change a commodity's price when it appears the supply will rise or fall as a result of new information.

Speculating on Commodity Prices

By far, the most widespread use of commodities futures is for speculative purposes. In financial market terminology, speculation can be defined as: the intentional assumption of usually short-term market risk based on the anticipation of an attractive return resulting from the expected price movement.

When it comes to commodities, the realm of speculation falls quite a bit beyond the general concept of investment, where an individual might acquire an asset in the expectation that it may appreciate like a stock or to take advantage of its return in terms of coupon yield and eventual redemption like a bond.

Instead, speculating on commodity futures seems considerably closer to gambling, which is the act of betting on an outcome without acquiring any assets. This is especially evident since approximately 97% of commodity futures do not go to physical delivery and are instead cash-settled.

The rest of this section covers why and how speculating on commodity prices takes place.

The Global Marketplace for Commodity Speculation

Speculating on commodity prices has become a huge business involving both small and large-scale commodity traders that usually operate through exchange-traded markets which are now positioned around the globe.

Although the U.S. commodity exchanges are especially well-known and highly-developed, other countries and regions such as India, Europe, China, South Africa and Australia have active commodity exchanges that now provide additional market depth, in addition to trading opportunities for speculators to take advantage of.

Why Speculation Helps Commodity Markets

Commodity speculators perform the useful service of providing liquidity and depth to the commodities market. Their presence also helps to prevent unwarranted price fluctuations, and can therefore help to maintain price stability in normal markets.

Nevertheless, in abnormal markets that often result from natural disasters, or times of economic and political instability, commodity speculation can fuel huge price swings in affected commodities. These speculative spikes, bubbles and crashes can cause significant aberrations in the marketplace experienced by consumers and producers alike.

Furthermore, most hedgers generally have a stake in the underlying commodity either as a producer, distributor or manufacturing user, and so they usually wish to employ futures contracts to protect against some form of commodity price risk.

Investors, on the other hand, tend to be considerably more common in the stock and bond markets, although investment in certain commodities like the precious metals is also fairly commonplace. The presence of commodity speculators helps both of these groups by increasing the overall liquidity of the commodity markets.

Speculators are Important Commodity Market Participants

Speculators make up an increasingly large share of participants in the commodities markets, and their participation has grown even further with the advent of online commodity trading. In fact, most people that now trade in the commodities market are speculators looking to enrich themselves from the price fluctuations seen in these huge and liquid marketplaces.

Other trading strategies that are commonly-used in the commodities markets include arbitrage between similar products trading in different markets and spreading between raw products and their derivatives, and.

As an example of spreading, the soybean complex can be considered an agricultural commodity system. In this system, when soybean futures are bought and soybean oil and meal futures are simultaneously sold in appropriate amounts, this will generally be known as a "crush spread" among commodity futures traders.

Nevertheless, the majority of trading activity occurs among speculators looking to profit from commodity price movements. In addition, most floor traders or "locals" on the commodities exchange floors are essentially speculators, with a few hedgers thrown into the mix.

Investing in Commodities

Some people initially approach the commodity market thinking that they can start investing in commodities, just as they can in other financial market assets like stocks and bonds. With the notable exception of investing over the long term or for retirement purposes in well-established stores of value like the precious metals, nothing could be further from the truth when it comes to the other commodities, since they are generally traded by individuals purely for speculative purposes.

It is vitally important that you realize that trading commodities is not an investment but is instead more of a strategic gambling game for speculators who enjoy taking risks. This is especially true if you do not happen to be a producer or industrial user who has a natural need to hedge against commodity price changes, often as a result of their underlying commodity production or consumption.

The rest of this section covers why people should think about how to speculate or trade commodities rather than looking for ways to start investing in commodities.

Commodity Market Participants

Now that you know you cannot really start investing in commodities, other than perhaps precious metals, it would probably make sense to clarify what the fuss on the Internet about commodity trading is all about. Well, first of all, the various commodities futures markets around the world together make up one of the largest markets in the world.

In the past, investment banks and other large commodity traders would sometimes get involved in the business of speculating on commodity price movements, but for the most part, the majority of commodity futures trading came about from those who were naturally interested in transacting commodities on either the buy or sell side.

In addition, some commodities market participants were interested in making commodities investment-related purchases as a result of their other business activities.

These days, this major marketplace has become increasingly available to the smaller commodities speculator as online trading has developed within the last ten years along with other electronic commodity trading platforms. Also, the increased availability of E-mini futures contracts on certain commodities has reduced minimum dealing amounts considerably.

As a result, this market that was once only readily accessible to large financial institutions, major commodity producers and users, and high-net worth individuals, has now become accessible to a much wider audience.

Online Trading Does Not Involve Investing in Commodities

Trading in the commodities market has expanded considerably along with the advent of the Internet and the subsequent rise of online commodity trading. Now, virtually anyone with a computer, an Internet connection, and the ability to install and run simple software programs can be up and running as a personal commodity trader taking commodity positions using E-mini futures contracts or Contracts for Difference (CFDs).

Of course, you still will not be investing in commodities. In fact, pretty much the only commodities-related investment you can make as a private individual will be in the commodity trading software you buy, the computer and Internet connection you need to run it on, and in the funds you put in your commodity trading account so that you can use them to speculate on commodity price fluctuations.

Trade Commodities; Don't Invest in Them!

Basically, the vast majority of commodity trading by individuals involves outright speculation, which is a strategic form of gambling. This is not commodities investment, other than perhaps when done in precious metals, and so it should only be engaged in by those who have funds to place at the risk of their complete loss.

Surely you would not think you were "investing" your bet on which football team wins the Superbowl or which horse comes out ahead in the big race? No, that sort of activity consists of gambling or speculation, and so does commodity trading.

As a result, if you were thinking of trying some casual commodity investing after reading about the commodity market online, and you were also hoping to keep your available funds safe for your retirement, perhaps commodity trading may not what you need at all.

Nevertheless, if you like to take strategic risks, think you might enjoy trying your hand at calling the direction of commodity price movements, and have funds available to place fully at risk, then trading commodities may be just the right thing for you.

Hedging Versus Speculating in Commodities

Hedging and speculating are two terms that are often used in commodities market terminology. Both represent an approach to commodities futures trading, although they are somewhat different in intention, implementation and results.

The rest of this section examines the difference between hedging and speculating in the commodities markets.

Hedging

The commodities markets in futures were originally created to "hedge" or insure against inclement weather in agricultural commodities. A farmer, unsure of the amount of a crop to be harvested in the fall, would typically buy a futures contract just in case his harvest did not produce what the farmer had already committed to delivering.

If the crop proved abundant, the farmer could sell the futures contract for a loss that would be offset by the crop the farmer had successfully harvested. On the other hand if the crop turned out to be below expectations, the farmer would make up for the loss on the crop by taking delivery of the futures contract or by selling the futures contract for a profit.

On the other hand, if the farmer or agricultural co-op expected a bumper crop, they might sell futures contracts to ensure a fair price before the effects of a large supply of the commodity made prices drop. The farmer could then give notice the buyer to take delivery of the commodity, thereby hedging his risk and having an outlet for the commodity at the same time.

Hedging with futures has been practiced with all types of commodities, not just agricultural commodities, and remains a viable strategy for producers as well as consumers of different commodities. Nevertheless, offsetting trades before the delivery date is often opted for, regardless of the hedge, which at least partially explains why roughly 97% of futures contracts get liquidated without delivery of the underlying commodity ever taking place.

Speculation

By far the most widespread use of commodities futures is for the purposes of speculation. In financial terms, speculation can be defined as the purposeful assumption of short-term economic risk with the expectation of an above-average return from an anticipated price change.

Commodity speculation therefore has less in common with investment, where one acquires an asset in expectation of its appreciation, and more in common with gambling, which is the betting on an outcome without acquiring any assets.

Speculators in the commodities market provide liquidity and depth and also prevent unwarranted fluctuations, maintaining stability in normal markets. In abnormal markets that can result from a natural disaster or economic and political instability, speculation can fuel wild price swings that unsettle commodity markets.

Together, hedgers and speculators make up the majority of participants in commodities markets. Investors tend to be much more prevalent in the stock and bond markets, although investment in certain commodities like the precious metals is also commonplace.

Basically, since a hedger needs something to hedge against, most people that participate in the commodities market are speculators looking to enrich themselves from the fluctuations in the market. While other strategies are used in commodities markets such as spreading, the majority of commodity trading activity happens among speculators.

Hedging Commodity Risk

If you are reading this book, then you are probably much more interested in trading commodities than in protecting against adverse commodity price movements that would be considered hedging activity. Nevertheless, even a trader should understand why producers and consumers of commodities may need to hedge their commodity price risks

The practice of hedging commodity risk has been around for a long time. In fact, the commodities futures markets were originally created to help agricultural commodity producers like farmers "hedge" or insure against weather and pest-related risks to their business of growing plants for food.

Basically, poor weather can significantly reduce the supply and hence increase the price of agricultural commodities until a new growing season can compensate to meet demand. Furthermore, good weather can often increase the supply of agricultural commodities and therefore lower their price until the excess supply eventually dwindles.

The rest of this section covers some of the reasons for hedging commodity risk and how producers typically do so using commodity futures.

Hedge Short Exposures with a Long Futures Contract

For example, a farmer not sure of the amount of a crop they might be harvesting in the fall would typically buy a futures contract on the agricultural item they produce. This would be done in order to protect against the situation in which the farmer's harvest did not produce what the farmer had already committed to delivering to their regular customers.

If the farmer's crop proved abundant, the farmer could then sell the futures contract that was originally purchased for a loss. The loss taken would then be offset by the increase in the crop that the farmer had successfully harvested and was now going to be able to distribute for additional gains.

On the other hand, if the crop produced in the fall turned out to be below the farmer's initial expectations, the farmer would then be able to make up for the loss experienced as a result of the poor crop by taking delivery of the product using the futures contract they had bought in order to satisfy the customers who had already been promised the produce.

Furthermore, if they had not pre-sold the produce, then they could also regain a least a portion of their losses by selling the futures contract they had purchased for a profit before the futures were scheduled to be delivered into.

Hedge Long Exposures with a Short Futures Contract

The farmer or agricultural co-op might choose to hedge against commodity price risk using a short futures contract. They might do this if they expected a bumper crop to be harvested in the fall and would do so by selling a futures contract or contracts on the estimated amount they expect to produce.

In this way, they can better ensure a fair price before the price-depressing effects of an excess supply of the commodity were felt and made wholesale prices drop. The farmer could then give notice to the buyer of the commodity futures contract that they will need to arrange to take physical delivery of the commodity. In this way, they are able to hedge against the risk of a price fall and also have an outlet for the commodity so that it will not go to waste in a market glut.

Hedging Commodity Risk with Futures is Increasingly Popular

Basically, hedging with futures contracts can now be practiced with just about all types of commodities, not just agricultural commodities. Furthermore, hedging commodity risk with futures is a viable and increasing popular strategy for both producers as well as consumers of the different commodities for which futures are readily traded.

Nevertheless, many commodity hedgers prefer to offset their futures trades before the delivery date. They often do so to avoid going through the challenges involved in taking physical delivery of a large quantity of a commodity that can result in storage and transportation fees.

This partially explains why roughly 97% of futures contracts will eventually be liquidated before delivery and the resulting gains or losses realized in cash without any actual delivery of the physical commodity ever occurring.

CHAPTER 2: THE COMMODITY MARKET

In order to trade commodities for your own account, you will first need to gain access to the markets in which their derivatives are bought and sold. Derivatives are financial products or contracts that have their value determined by the value or price of an underlying asset. In the case of commodities, the most commonly traded derivatives are futures, options and Contracts for Difference or CFDs.

The following section discusses the global commodity market and mentions what the principal world commodity exchanges are, how trading takes place on those exchanges, and what commodity types currently trade on each exchange.

Global Commodity Exchanges

Global commodity trading has grown exponentially in recent years with the growing human population, online commodity trading and other contributing factors. Commodities exchanges are now being established in many commodities-producing countries and this has resulted in commodity trading becoming an increasingly global pastime.

In addition to the world commodities exchanges, a number of U.S. exchanges have recently consolidated due to the advent of electronic and online commodity trading, thereby creating the largest commodities trading complex in the world.

The United States' and European commodities exchanges account for the lion's share of commodities futures trading worldwide. Nevertheless, an increasing number of other commodities exchanges throughout the world also actively trade commodities futures.

Many of the commodities that trade in other exchanges around the world are not found on either U.S.-based or European commodities exchanges, and they are often produced in the region where the exchanges are located. Some of these exchanges are listed below along with their location and featured commodities.

A partial list of global commodity trading exchanges and the types of commodities traded on each one follows:

The Americas

- **The Chicago Mercantile Exchange** – The "Merc" or CME originally started as the Chicago Butter and Egg Board in 1898 and changed its name to the Chicago Mercantile Exchange in 1919 when it expanded commodity trading to other products. In 2007, the exchange merged with the Chicago Board of Trade, the largest grains market in the world and changed its name to the CME Group.

    In 2008, the CME Group merged with the New York Mercantile Exchange or NYMEX which had already merged with the COMEX or Commodities Exchange of New York. The CME Group also has the Globex and ClearPort electronic commodity trading platforms where commodities futures are traded around the clock, Sunday thru Friday.

    This single commodities exchange is now responsible for 90% of all commodities futures traded in the United States, covering just about every type of commodity from crude oil and precious metals, to livestock, grains, coffee and cocoa, and thereby encompassing virtually all of the commodities actively traded in the United States.

- **The Winnipeg Commodity Exchange** - now forms part of the International Commodities Exchange or ICE and is now known as ICE Futures Canada. The exchange was founded in 1887 and is Canada's only commodities futures exchange. The exchange is fully-electronic and was the first exchange to convert to an electronic trading platform. The commodities traded on the exchange include feed wheat, rapeseed or canola, and western barley.

- **The Brazilian Mercantile and Futures Exchange** (BM&F) – was created as a merger between the Bolsa de Valores, Mercadorias y Futuros de São Paulo or BOVESPA to create BM&FBOVESPA. This is the fourth largest exchange in the Americas as far as market capitalization is concerned, and it is both a commodities futures exchange and a stock exchange. The exchange trades commodities such as orange juice futures and grain.

- **The Rosario Board of Trade** – also known as the Bolsa de Comercio de Rosario is an Argentine commodities exchange founded in 1884 in the Province of Santa Fe, Argentina. The commodities futures traded on this exchange include those on grain and other agricultural products, such as oilseed and the soybean complex.

Europe

- **Euronext.liffe** – the result of the 2002 merger of the London International Financial Futures and Options Exchange (LIFFE) and the Euronext Exchange. The Euronext was composed of the Paris, Brussels, Lisbon and Amsterdam derivatives exchanges which merged. While commodity trading is not as active on this exchange as trading in securities and interest-rate futures, Euronext.liffe has become the largest European exchange for trading commodities.

- **The London Metal Exchange** (LME) – the world's largest options and futures exchange for trading commodities like precious and base metals. Also, the LME allows for cash-settled trading, in addition to providing the option of physical delivery for contract settlement.

Asia

- **The Dalian Commodity Exchange** (DCE) – The largest commodities exchange in China was established in 1993 as a non-profit and self-regulating futures exchange that is now considered one of the largest agricultural futures exchange in the world. The DCE trades grains and palm oil futures, as well as plastics products and steel futures, among other products.

- **The National Multi-Commodity Exchange of India Limited** (NMCE) – an India-based electronic commodities exchange that has been in operation since 2002. The exchange trades futures on commodities such as grains, spices, oil seeds, cash crops, precious metals and base metals.

- **The National Commodity and Derivatives Exchange Limited** (NCDEX) - an online commodity trading exchange based in India which trades over 57 commodities that include spices, edible oils, precious metals, plastics and cotton among others.

- **The Multi Commodity Exchange** (MCX) – also located in India, the MCX is an independent commodity trading exchange based in Mumbai that is the largest commodities exchange in India and accounts for over 80% of that market's volume share. The MCX is also the world's largest exchange for silver futures, and daily trading volume in all commodities exceeds U.S. $2.4 billion.

The Middle East

- **The Dubai Mercantile Exchange** (DME) – the largest commodity trading exchange in the East of Suez region for energy-related commodities futures. The exchange's main product is the Oman Crude Oil Futures Contract which is a benchmark for Middle Eastern crude oil.

- **The Iranian Oil Bourse** – also known as the Iran Petroleum Exchange and the Oil Bourse in Kish, is a commodity exchange specializing in oil and energy products that trade in currencies other than the U.S. Dollar, and primarily denominated in the Euro and the Iranian Rial. The exchange is located on the Persian Gulf island of Kish.

How Commodities Trade

Understanding the commodities market and how commodities trade is important to anyone who plans on trading commodities. It can also be of interest to those who wish to understand how modern commodities trading and hedging works. The rest of this section discusses how commodities trade.

Commodity Trading in Practice

In practice, most commodities are traded using futures contracts on an exchange floor, such as those of the Chicago Mercantile Exchange and the others mentioned in the previous section. Commodities can also be traded on electronic dealing systems that access those exchange traded markets, or in the over the counter commodities market. Options on futures and forward contracts are typically also available.

Due to the large minimum transaction sizes and other barriers to entry, trading via these venues is typically only accessible to higher net worth individuals, producers, hedgers, exchange floor traders and the large financial institutions that make markets.

Some popular commodities can also be traded via Contracts for Difference or CFDs, which are a form of derivative that is priced based on the price of the underlying commodity. Trading in CFDs is generally offered by online brokers using margin accounts, and CFD trades are executed using an electronic trading platform like MetaTrader.

Due to the low barrier to entry involved in CFD trading, this type of trading is most appropriate for smaller retail speculators and can often be commenced by placing a modest margin deposit with an online broker and downloading free trading software.

Exchange-Traded Commodities

Commodity exchanges were based around groups of traders that would meet at specific places to trade commodities that later became the first exchanges. Commodity exchanges started in different cities around the United States, Europe and elsewhere, although they have become more centralized in recent years in large cities like Chicago, for example.

With the advent of electronic trading, much of the trading in commodities has become electronic, even on the exchange floors. Many customer orders are now automatically executed on the exchange's trading platform, rather than via the traditional open outcry method.

While a large portion of commodity trading execution is now automated on the exchange floors, several basic manual elements of commodity trading continue despite the automation of many of the exchange's functions.

Typically, the commodity exchange operates by having market-makers that specialize in making two-way prices in a specific commodity future contract. Their two-way price or "market" consists of both an offered price at which subsequent investors can buy the contract, as well as a bid price at which those who already own the commodity contract can sell what they already have or go short.

On commodity exchanges, futures contracts are typically offered for a series of standardized delivery dates and options on those futures contracts are usually offered at a range of strike prices around the prevailing market price. Also associated with commodity exchanges are brokers who enter orders for clients. Clients of the exchanges are typically traders or hedgers.

The markets in exchange traded commodities are among the largest markets in the world and commodities enjoy a certain prestige in being listed on the Chicago Mercantile Exchange or CME, as well as increased market liquidity. Nevertheless, times have changed, and most commodities also trade electronically, as well as on other regional exchanges like those listed in the previous section.

Over-The-Counter and Electronically-Traded Commodities

Even though commodities have been traded over-the-counter for many years, the advent of the electronic age has made the over-the-counter market vastly more efficient. It now makes use of electronic trading platforms, in addition to the traditional telephone network that commodity traders and market makers formerly used to trade over-the-counter on.

In addition to the over-the-counter market, a number of Electronic Communication Networks or ECN's also participate in the trading of commodities, and these provide an alternative for both OTC and exchange-traded commodity markets.

Online Commodity Trading

Over the last twenty years, a number of online broking firms have emerged which have evolved into major players in the world of commodity trading and typically cater to smaller retail traders.

Many online broking firms exist today, and their success reflects the general trend towards automation and electronic trading platforms.

Basically, open outcry commodity exchanges are gradually becoming obsolete as traders increasingly move to electronic trading formats facilitated by Internet communications.

Furthermore, quite a few commodity exchanges continue to have commodities futures contracts listed and allow electronic trading even though they no longer have a physical exchange floor location for open outcry trading.

Commodity trading has evolved considerably over the last forty years thanks to the rise of computers and the Internet. The next three decades will most likely see even more technological advancements affecting how commodities trade.

Trading Commodities Online

Trading commodities was not the same before the advent of electronic trading via the Internet. The only way a person could even get a commodity quote was by calling a commodity futures broker, and then you had to be a customer in order to be given a quote.

Today, you can just type the name of a commodity into a search engine in your Internet browser, and the results will include a link that will provide a real time price quote on the commodity. In addition, a sizeable database with technical and fundamental information on all major and minor commodities that are publicly traded can be obtained from many online brokers and other information providers via the Internet.

Trading commodities over the Internet has gained an enormous following in recent years, with thousands of people currently trading commodities online. If you have no previous commodity trading experience, many online brokers also now offer demo accounts, where you can practice using their trading platform software and trading commodities. Such demo accounts are also very useful for testing a trading plan.

Perhaps the best way to decide which broker's trading platform is best is by checking each one out that appears on your short list of online brokers. You will want to look for one that has the most user-friendly package and whose trading platform fits your needs best.

Also, trading online has become so popular recently that even many full-service futures brokerages now also offer online packages and trading platforms for their clients. This has made trading commodities over the Internet available to just about anyone with the funds to invest and a reasonably modern computer capable of getting online.

With the advent of electronic commodity trading via the Internet, a trader can now probably implement their commodity trade plan on an online trading platform that may even allow automation. Also, depending on the broker selected, a trader may even be able to get a free trading platform to execute trades with that they can install on their computer or smartphone or use via a Web browser of their choice.

Furthermore, if a trader is planning on dealing via an online broker, then they will probably be trading Contracts for Difference or CFDs rather than commodity futures themselves. From a trader's perspective, there is typically little practical difference when it comes to pricing between a CFD and a futures contract, since the CFD is priced based on the price of the underlying commodity, just as the futures contract is, although there may be a modest difference due to costs of carrying a commodity for a future delivery date. Basically, a CFD on a commodity is a commodity derivative and not the commodity itself, in much the same way as a futures contract is.

The following sections cover what a commodity trading platform is, how it is used as a commodity trading system and which types of broker might offer a free commodity trading platform.

Advantages of Trading Commodities Online

The fact that the Internet provides a world of resources right at one's fingertips makes up one of the best reasons to trade commodities online. With real-time news and information on the financial markets streaming twenty-four hours a day, information related to individual commodities has now become available to investors almost as it happens.

Getting information on the commodity market in today's Information Age has come a long way since the time when Nathan Rothschild once took advantage of the information obtained from his secret network that Napoleon had lost at Waterloo to make a killing on the London Stock Exchange from those who thought he had instead won the decisive battle.

In addition to the real-time information stream, commodity traders can also take advantage of sophisticated trading platforms that online brokers have developed for their customers. Such trading platforms often contain numerous tools and resources which can be extremely useful to commodity traders, like price charts to perform technical analysis with, for example.

Commodity Futures Trading

If you have ever witnessed the way commodity futures are traded on an exchange floor, you might get the impression that the crowds of people shouting and gesticulating have all gone crazy. Nothing could be further from the truth.

Although most trading volume these days takes place via electronic systems, commodity futures still trade by open outcry on some exchanges. Open outcry, in commodity futures trading terminology, refers to the buying and selling of commodity futures contracts by shouting bids and offers in a crowd of traders in a pit. Traders then use hand signals to execute and further confirm trades.

The rest of this section covers how trading commodity futures is commonly done on the commodity exchange floor.

Buying Commodity Futures

When a commodity trader in a ring or pit, as the tiered areas on the exchange floor where trading takes place are called, is buying futures contracts, they will follow a certain protocol to alert other traders to the fact that they are a buyer.

First, the trader will stand in the pit facing the crowd with hands towards their body. This will indicate that they are buying and not selling. Second, they will shout the price they are willing to pay for the contracts followed by the amount of contracts upon which they are bidding.

For example, the trader would shout "four on twenty... four on twenty," which would indicate that the commodity futures trader is bidding a price of four on twenty contracts. The ring or pit will have designated areas for the different contract months, so the location of the trader in the pit will indicate what month contracts they are buying.

As the trader is shouting "four on twenty," a seller across the pit will signal to the trader that they are willing to sell ten contracts at four which they will confirm with hand gestures and subsequently write on a ticket. The commodity futures trader nearest the exchange reporting clerk will tell the clerk "four trade" and the price will be reported to the exchange through a transmitter and will immediately show as the last sale on the commodity price board.

The buying trader will continue shouting in the pit, although now he will shout "four on ten" because he has already bought ten contracts. Depending on how the trader feels about the market action, they may either buy an offer, up their bid or stop bidding altogether.

Selling Commodity Futures

The above procedure is reversed when selling. The trader will stand in the pit with hands away from the body indicating they are a seller. Instead of shouting the price first, however the seller will state the quantity of contracts for sale first, followed by the price.

Instead of shouting "four on twenty" as the buyer in the previous example was shouting, the seller will instead shout "twenty at five…twenty at five." Again, if another commodity futures trader is willing to pay the offer, they will signal the seller to buy whatever amount they are bidding for. The process is repeated until the seller's interest is satisfied.

The Efficiency of the Open Outcry Method of Trading

This open outcry exchange trading process is surprisingly efficient. Furthermore, commodities and other financial instruments have been traded in this fashion since the 19th century. Commodity futures continue to be traded this way at the present time, despite the rise of electronic commodity trading methods.

Basically, having a sizeable group of local traders trading for their own account in a centralized exchange adds liquidity and depth to the market, and is one of the main reasons behind the open outcry system's success.

The Commodity Futures Exchange Floor

Trading commodities on a commodities exchange floor involves knowledge of trading floor protocol and etiquette. Floor trading has traditionally been done by "locals" who are independent traders and floor brokers that trade for their own and for customer's accounts.

The rest of this section discusses the commodity futures exchange floor, market participants and general commodities exchange information.

Exchange Floor Participants

If you have ever visited a commodities exchange using the open outcry method of trading, the activity on the trading floor often resembles chaotic activity with floor traders, floor brokers and other participants waving and gesticulating wildly. While it may seem chaotic to an outsider, this sort of commodities exchange action is actually quite organized.

In addition to the main participants who are actively trading, a large group of support staff and clerks are also a key element in the efficient running of a commodities exchange. The main trading participants on a commodities exchange floor are locals and brokers.

Locals

The traders that make up the majority of the crowd in the ring or pit as the tiered circle is commonly referred to are the locals. The locals are generally independent traders buying and selling commodity futures for their own account.

The locals are exchange members who have purchased a "seat" or membership on the exchange. Some members lease seats from other members as seats can be extremely expensive. Nevertheless, a person can become a member without owning a seat.

All members are tested on exchange floor protocol and general exchange floor operations before being allowed to trade. In addition, a minimum capital requirement is necessary to begin trading futures contracts on the floor.

Floor Brokers

In addition to the locals, another group of members who can also participate as locals and buy and sell for their own account are the floor brokers. Floor brokers typically fill customer orders from people off of the exchange floor who cannot execute their own orders, as well as for other exchange members that cannot be physically present to execute their own orders.

The floor broker will receive the orders either via a ticket handed to them by a "runner," an employee of a member clearing firm who distributes orders written on tickets to the floor broker, or by a hand signal from a phone clerk. The phone clerk will use special hand signals to indicate buy or sell and the quantity and price of the order. Typically, another clerk in the employ of the floor broker will receive the order, write it down and then hand it to the floor broker.

Clearing Trades

One of the reasons that commodity futures exchanges seem so efficient has to do with them having a strictly-regulated centralized clearing procedure for all trades. All trades must be announced immediately after execution and reported to an exchange employee. They, in turn, generally report the trade to the exchange's Time and Sales Department, thereby making a record of the trade and when it was executed.

After this, the ticket is submitted to the exchange which will guarantee all commodity futures trades go through the clearing process. In other words all buys and sells are automatically offset by a central clearing corporation that takes the credit risk from the individual traders.

All clearing firms will then credit and debit the individual accounts where the trades take place. This clearing process results in a smoother trading operation where literally billions of dollars in commodity futures trades can be executed daily.

Finer Points of Trading Commodities Futures

In commodities futures trading, the great majority of outstanding contracts, estimated at over 97%, are offset before the delivery date. One primary reason for this involves the relative ease for traders, producers and consumers of commodities to offset their original futures positions instead of opting to take physical delivery.

Conversely, some traders who are producers or who consume the particular commodity in question will invariably take physical delivery. They seek to deliver the commodity before the last trading date in order to fulfill the contract.

The rest of this section explains some of the finer points of commodity trading for future delivery and how commodities futures sellers notice buyers to expect physical delivery of the commodity.

Terms of Delivery

Each commodities exchange sets the terms for physical delivery of a commodity futures contract traded on their trading floor or electronic trading platform, as well as the schedule upon which such deliveries take place.

The exchange must give notice to the party expected to take delivery, and it generally uses two types of notices that are either transferable or non-transferable.

Transferable Notices

A transferable notice is issued through the Clearing House, which is the entity in charge of guaranteeing the trading of all contracts, from the seller to the buyer of the commodities futures contract. The notice advises the buyer of the seller's intention to deliver the commodity to satisfy the futures contract.

Once the buyer has received the notice, the buyer has the option of either taking delivery of the commodity or of offsetting the futures contract on the exchange's trading floor in a process called re-tendering. This effectively transfers the notice to another party.

Commodity traders need to be aware that exchanges generally only give buyers a limited time to pass on the transferable notices. Typically, this time runs between 45 minutes to an hour after receipt of the notice, although some exchanges will allow contracts to be re-tendered on the next business day.

Non-Transferable Notices

The Clearing House also takes responsibility for giving the commodity futures contract buyer non-transferable notices on behalf of the seller. These let the buyer know that the seller has the intention of delivering the commodity physically in order to satisfy the commodities futures contract.

If the buyer receives the notice before the last trading day for the contract, they can sell another futures contract against the delivery. Nevertheless, all costs of ownership for the time the buyer is in possession of the commodity, typically one to three days, will be incurred by the buyer. These might include storage, spoilage and any transport costs.

Seller's Option Versus Cash-Settled Futures

In general, most contracts for commodities are seller's option contracts. This means that the seller has the option to deliver the commodity physically to the buyer of the contract on the standardized delivery date. On the other hand, buyers cannot demand delivery from the contract sellers.

Nevertheless, some commodity futures contracts are cash-settled. These contracts do not involve a physical delivery option, but this is not the norm in the commodities market.

First and Last Notice Days

The commodities exchange which issues the commodities futures contracts takes responsibility for designating the first day which a seller may tender a notice to a buyer. This is typically called the First Notice Day, and it begins the physical delivery process.

The First Notice Day for most commodities is usually three business days before the first business day of the delivery month. In order to avoid taking physical delivery, a trader must liquidate their long position prior to the First Notice Day.

The Last Notice Day represents the last day a commodities future seller may tender a delivery notice to a buyer. This date usually falls from two to seven business days before the last day of the delivery month.

Last Trading Day

The last day for trading a commodities futures contract is known as the Last Trading Day. In general, all futures contracts outstanding after the last trading day must be satisfied by the physical delivery of the underlying commodity, if they are not cash-settled futures. The last trading day varies depending on the commodity and the exchange it is traded on.

Trading Commodities Over the Counter

In the world of commodities markets, trading commodities over-the-counter does not happen as often as trading commodities futures on commodity exchanges. Over-the-counter commodities are normally traded with forward contracts.

The rest of this section offers some details about what over-the-counter trading is, what it entails and how it differs from commodity futures trading.

Over-the-Counter versus Exchange-Traded Commodities

In market terminology, "over-the-counter" or OTC refers to

transactions that are performed off of the floor of the centralized stock and commodities exchanges, and generally in a private transaction between two parties. In many cases, the two parties to the OTC transaction are an investment bank or other financial institution and one of its clients.

Commodities for immediate delivery are traded on the OTC spot market, and OTC forward contracts are also available for longer delivery dates. An over-the-counter forward contract differs from an exchange traded futures contract in that the over-the-counter contract is a non-standardized, bilateral contract between two parties for a given amount of a specified commodity for delivery at a pre-determined future date for an agreed-upon price.

On the other hand, an exchange-traded commodities futures contract provides buyers and sellers with standardized contracts for a uniform-quality commodity. These contracts also have a series of specific, periodic delivery dates, which are typically every month for many commodities.

While exchange-traded commodities futures require an initial deposit or margin to trade, over-the-counter forward contracts are paid for and settled upon delivery. Many over-the-counter contracts therefore either require credit to be extended, or they include provisions for collateral in the event of the commodity price change adversely affecting one of the parties.

In addition, over-the-counter commodities forward contracts contain other provisions in the event of a default by either the buyer or seller of the contract, with specific re-imbursement granted to either party if the other one cannot meet their obligations under the contract.

Size of the Over-The-Counter Commodities Market

The amount of commodities forward contracts that trade over-the-counter make up less than two percent of commodities trading overall. Because of the lack of standardization both in the size of the contracts, as well as the uncertainty as to the quality of the underlying product, over-the-counter commodities forward contracts have not been a popular way to trade commodities. Nevertheless, they do allow hedgers to protect specific harvest dates, for example.

The main participants in the over-the-counter commodities forward market are the large investment banks and other financial institutions. Such institutions are adequately-capitalized and can therefore afford to enter into over-the-counter commodities forward contracts with their clients because they have the capacity to offset their risk either with other over-the-counter forwards or with exchange-traded futures.

The majority of all over-the-counter commodities forwards are transacted in the precious metals. The precious metals market lends itself well to the needs of investment banks and is also the market that the banks' hedging and speculating customers most frequently choose to trade with customized forward contracts.

Over-The-Counter Forwards or Exchange-Traded Futures

Basically, unless you have a particular need for a customized forward contract on a particular commodity, you are generally much better off trading exchange traded futures versus over-the-counter forwards.

One of the major drawbacks of the over-the-counter commodities forward market is the relative lack of liquidity. Once you enter into the forward contract, regardless of how the market behaves, you will most likely have to offset the position with the bank you initially dealt with, or wind up taking physical delivery of the commodity.

While this may be just what some commodity producers require, for the majority of speculative commodities traders, the over-the-counter forward makes very little sense. If you think you have a need for this type of commodity trading arrangement, talk to your investment banker about their over-the-counter commodities trading.

Commodity Options

Commodity options are similar to options on shares of stock or even real estate in that they confer upon the commodities option buyer the right, but not the obligation, to enter into a contract with the seller at a particular price. Naturally, the option owner pays a price or "premium" for this right, and they generally exercise their right only when it is to their financial advantage.

Commodity options have gained widespread acceptance as invaluable tools for managing commodity price risk, and they currently make up a significant percentage of commodity market turnover.

Not only is the commodities option market actively-traded among large futures traders and major commodity producers and users, but it is also increasingly available to smaller, personal commodity speculators and hedgers due to the rise of online commodity trading.

Although the Chicago and New York Mercantile Exchanges have offered commodity options in fairly small lot sizes for years for standardized delivery dates and strike prices, obtaining prices and dealing online is a relatively recent phenomenon that has greatly reduced the start-up costs involved in commodities option trading.

While an in depth discussion of option trading is beyond the scope of this book, the rest of this section provides an introduction and a basic overview of the commodities option market that includes how commodity options are specified, priced and used to manage risk.

Characteristics and Pricing of Commodity Options

A commodities option has similar characteristics to an option on a stock because its underlying contract typically involves a certain amount of the commodity and its value fluctuates along with the price of the commodity. Furthermore, if you want to establish a long position in a commodity using a commodities option, you would purchase the right to buy or "call" that commodity. Conversely, if you wish to establish a short position, you would buy the right to sell or "put" that commodity.

Commodity options differ from stock and forex options due to the fact that the underlying commodities generally do not have either interest rates like currencies or dividends like stocks. Commodities can however have costs involved in storing or borrowing them, so such factors may be fed into the option price and can especially impact longer term options.

Accordingly, the main observable market parameters used to price commodity options include the prevailing commodity spot or futures price and the level of implied volatility corresponding to a particular commodity and time frame.

In addition to which commodity is to be bought or sold in the underlying futures contract, additional commodity option contract specifications affect their pricing. These extra factors include the:

- Transaction or "strike" price,
- Maturity or "expiration" date of the option
- Delivery Date of the underlying commodity futures or forward contract.

Executing and Exercising Commodity Options

When it comes to executing a commodity option transaction, the parties involved will first specify an underlying futures or forward contract. The buyer of the option will be granted the right, but not the obligation, to enter into that specified contract in the direction and at the price they require for a fee or premium.

The buyer can exercise their right during (for American-style options) or at the end of (for European-style options) a pre-specified time period, the end of which is known as the maturity date. Most exchange-traded commodity options are American-style.

Managing Commodity Risk Using Commodity Options

Not only does a commodities option offer a unique risk profile, but commodity options can also be used in various combinations involving commodity options of different maturity dates and strike prices.

This feature allows a strategic commodity trader or hedger to create a customized option strategy and risk profile that precisely matches their particular needs and market view for that commodity's price.

These desirable characteristics of commodity options considerably broaden the range of commodity hedging and trading alternatives available to the commodity risk managers, strategic commodity traders and commodity producers and consumers who use them. Fortunately, various choices exist for those interested in trading commodity options online.

CHAPTER 3: GETTING STARTED TRADING COMMODITIES

For those sincerely interested in getting started trading commodities for their own account, the good news is that you can easily start out doing so with even a modest initial deposit by trading commodity CFDs as an online trader in a margin account.

On the other hand, if you wish to become a professional commodity trader working for a major international bank on a top-notch salary or on a futures exchange floor, then your chances of success are much slimmer and the competition truly fierce.

As a result, this chapter will focus primarily on supporting the first type of aspiring do-it-yourself commodity trader who will be speculating on commodity market movements with their own funds in a margin account.

A Trader Learning Action Plan

In addition to reading this book, developing expertise in trading commodities by practicing and doing online research at reputable websites in the following general areas is highly recommended.

You can also use the following four step learning action plan as a way to direct the progress of your commodity trading education:

- **Step #1: Learn Commodity Trading Mechanics**

You will first want to make sure you have the commodity trading basics under your belt. This means that you have set up an account with a futures broking firm or an online broker; you have phone access to a futures broker or an electronic trading platform that can execute transactions; and that you know how to enter and exit commodity positions.

You will also need to know about the different types of orders that your broker permits, how to enter them, and when to use them appropriately. Also, each commodity futures contract will have its own specifications, so be sure to read and understand them thoroughly to prevent undesirable errors due to your ignorance.

Many brokers and even futures exchanges offer some valuable information about commodity trading and contract details on their websites, so make sure to take advantage of those resources.

- **Step #2: Learn How Fundamentals Move the Market**

Basically, commodity price movements occur in dynamic response to the situations and events either occurring or widely-predicted for the commodity, its producers and users. Fundamental factors that can affect a commodity's price may include relevant economic data releases, the level of inflation and interest rates, weather reports, production supply and industrial demand factors, and legislative changes.

As market participants shift their expectations to encompass such new information, and their positions accordingly, the net result is that the supply/demand balance shifts to a higher or lower price for the commodity. To accurately predict future price changes, one therefore needs to take into account fundamental information pertaining to both the commodity and also to the currency it is most actively traded in.

You will also want to have access to a good-quality economic data calendar with consensus expectations and release times listed for the numbers due to be released and key upcoming events like elections and central bank rate decisions. Watching the weather reports for key agricultural production areas can also be important for soft commodity pricing.

It is also a good idea to research online what the relevant fundamental factors mean to the commodity market you are trading, and their relative importance in terms of market-moving potential. Keep in mind that even major commodity markets can be illiquid, with wider spreads and sharper moves often seen during the release of important data.

Furthermore, since you probably will not be privy to information about the large transaction flows that move the commodity market, you will want to develop an understanding of why those flows might occur and what factors the big commodity producers, industrial users, market makers and traders employ to shift their sense of a commodity's valuation and hence its market price.

- **Step #3: Learn to Trade Commodities Using Technical Analysis**

Due to the fact that your fundamental information flow may be inferior to that taken advantage of by the larger commodity market players, one thing you can reasonably be assured of knowing is the current price for a commodity and how it has fluctuated in the past. Having a good price charting system, with a reliable historical data stream is vital here.

Armed with that price data information, you will then need to take the time to become proficient at using the many methods of technical analysis can help you utilize this information to predict the overall direction and even the level of future commodity prices.

- **Step #4: Develop a Commodity Trading Plan and Stick to It**

One of the classic trading adages passed down by seasoned traders to novices learning the ropes of trading markets is to "Plan your trade, and trade your plan."

By using reliable technical analysis signals and other important market observables to set up your trading entry and exit points in an objective way, you can much more easily avoid many of the emotionally-based pitfalls that can blow out margin trading accounts.

Trading commodities often becomes a much more enjoyable and often considerably more profitable experience if you can just find the disciple needed to stick to your trade plan.

Choosing a Commodities Broker

Trading commodities involves several preliminary steps that every commodity trader needs to know to successfully make commodity transactions. The first step consists of course in getting a reputable broker to act as your intermediary when executing commodity transactions.

Some of the initial things you will need to ascertain before getting a commodity broker includes what your needs are and what type of trading you intend to be doing. The first item can easily be determined by considering whether your needs are for hedging purposes or for short-term speculation. As a general rule, most retail traders will be speculating on commodity price movements and not hedging.

The rest of this section discusses what a person needs to know about how to trade commodities via a broker, including what commodities to consider trading, whether to choose futures or CFDs and what brokers offer those commodity trading products, getting a reputable broker, and what issues to consider when choosing a broker.

Selecting What Commodities to Trade and Why

Before choosing a broker and funding a margin account with them, you will first want to think about what kind of commodities you should consider trading. This important question can be readily answered by assessing your trading objectives as follows:

- **Speculation** – this type of trading will take considerable effort and attention and will generally be done by an individual or a hedge fund. You will also be taking risks with your money that could result in its complete loss. If you are inclined to be more speculative, actively traded commodities will provide ample volatility for short-term speculation. Almost any commodity with a reasonable amount of volatility and market access can be traded by a speculator. Most smaller individual and retail speculators will find CFD trading adequate for their needs and more modest preferred transaction sizes, while larger speculators like hedge funds and high net worth individuals might need to access the futures or OTC markets to handle their more substantial transaction volumes.

- **Commercial Need** – if you are a producer or industrial user of commodities, then the futures market will probably offer the sort of larger transaction sizes you will require to protect or hedge your business' exposure to commodity price changes. You will therefore need to contact a futures broker.

- **Investment** – if your objective in getting involved with commodities is to acquire them for long term investment and perhaps as a hedge against inflation, consider those that have consistent price growth potential, are a reliable store of wealth, have a limited supply and established demand, and have a relatively stable price history or an upward price trend. Precious metals like gold and silver tend to fit these descriptions and are therefore popular long term investments for both individual and institutional investors. If you live in the United States, you can even put precious metals in a self-directed Individual Retirement Account or IRA to enjoy its tax advantages. Most investors will opt for the cash or physical market and then obtain a storage facility or custodian for the commodity they purchase, or they might invest in commodity-linked Exchange Traded Funds to obtaining exposure to a commodity or basket of commodities for investment purposes.

Getting a Broker

If you plan on trading commodity futures without actually being situated on one of the futures exchange trading floors, then you will need to get a futures broker that can access those markets for you. Most retail traders will want to simply start a relationship with an online broker that offers CFD trading in the commodities they are interested in trading.

In either situation, you will probably have no need for a full service broker like many stock market investors use since you will generally be doing your own research and making your own trading decisions.

Furthermore, if your primary trading goal is to profit from short-term commodity price moves, an online CFD broker with the best dealing spreads in the commodities you are interested in trading should be a better fit than a futures broker, especially if you only plan on dealing in modest amounts.

Another consideration when getting a broker is that if you sign up with a broker that also offers forex trading, you may also be able to trade the currencies, like the Australian, New Zealand and Canadian Dollars, which tend to move along with the prices of certain commodities.

Finally, most online brokers nowadays either offer support for MetaTrader or have their own impressive trading platforms with charting capabilities, news wires and other useful research tools, and even the ability to fully automate a trade plan.

Choosing Among Brokers

When choosing a broker for trading commodities, you will want to be sure that you select a reputable brokerage firm that will provide the best and most appropriate service available for the funds you have to deposit.

Remember, high brokerage fees and an inadequate trade execution service can be very costly in the fast-moving commodity market. The rest of this section discusses some common questions that should be answered during the process of choosing a reputable commodity broker.

The first step to take is to determine if you will want to trade commodity futures or CFDs as that will strongly influence your choice of brokers.

Once you have determined whether you will need a futures exchange or online broker, you will need to choose from among a fairly large selection. A few items to consider in the selection would be:

- **Experience and Reputation** – a good broker will have experience dealing with other clients, have been in business for a reasonable period of time, and have established a good reputation.

- **Commissions, Spreads and Fees** – commissions and/or dealing spreads can vary considerably among brokers, so look for competitive commissions and spreads that are a big plus — especially if you plan on trading frequently. Online brokers offering CFDs tend to have much lower commissions than futures brokers, and you will probably also have to pay exchange fees if you are planning on dealing in futures contracts.

- **Licenses and Regulations** – A good broker will be suitably licensed and regulated as required in their jurisdiction.

- **Fees** – many brokers charge additional fees for account management, including trading account deposits and withdrawals, so make sure you are clear with the prospective broker about this before making a decision.

The following subsections list several areas that include key account, security and trading considerations that you will probably want to investigate further before selecting a commodity broker. Each section also includes appropriate questions to ask on various important issues in order to get the answers you will need to make a better-informed decision when choosing a reputable commodity broker.

Key Commodity Broker Issues

- **Performance** - What is the commodity broker's reputation among their clients, and do they provide fast and accurate commodity trade executions of the type you prefer?

- **Broker Type** - Is the broker a futures broker or a CFD broker and is that type most suitable for your needs? Will they provide valuable services like assisting you with your education and making trading decisions? Do they offer you access to special research and information like a Reuters news feed or a trade signal service, or are they a discount broker offering lower commissions without the frills?

- **Trading Platform** - If the broker permits online trading, do you like the broker's trading platform and does it have the functionality you require, including supporting any automation needs you might have? Does the broker offer mobile trading solutions and alerts if you need such services?

- **Commodities and Products Offered** - Which commodities does the broker generally provide an execution service for and does that suit your needs? Also, do they let you trade a variety of products like futures, options, forwards and CFDs or just CFDs?

- **Leverage and Margin** - What sort of maximum leverage ratio does your broker provide, what is their margin call policy, and do they automatically stop trades out if insufficient margin is present in your account?

- **Trading Fees, Commissions, Dealing Spreads, and Payment Fees** - What trading fees, dealing spreads and/or commissions does the broker charge and under what conditions? Also, what payments fees are charged for fund transfers like margin account deposits and withdrawals?

- **Order Types and Slippage** - What types of orders does the broker support? Also, if your chosen trading strategy requires one-cancels-the-other (OCO) orders or trailing stops, does the broker offer these more complex order types? Does the broker guarantee that stop loss orders will be executed at the price they are placed at, or are you subject to order price slippage in especially active markets?

Key Broker Security Issues

- **Regulation -** What sort of regulation is the broker subject to, in what country and under what regulatory agency? Many futures and online CFD brokers are required to be regulated by Commodities Futures Trading Commission or CFTC in the United States. Make sure that this agency regulates the broker you choose if they are based in the United States or that they are regulated by other major regulatory agency if they are based in another country.

- **Fund Safety -** Is the broker well-capitalized, do they separate client funds from their own in case of bankruptcy and deposit them with a well-rated financial institution, and are client funds insured against loss? These are all very important questions to ask before sending any funds to a broker.

- **Data Security -** If you are considering an online CFD broker, you will probably be making personal financial transactions via the Internet or storing vital trading and account information online. In this case, you will want to know whether the broker has suitable protective measures in place to keep your data secure from loss, misuse or theft.

Key Broker Account Issues

- **Account Types -** Will the broker open an account of the type you want with the funds you currently have available to invest? Does the broker offer a margin account if you plan on trading on margin? What maximum leverage ratio do they permit traders to use? Do they support automated trading, if that is important to you?

- **Deposits and Withdrawals -** Does the broker support making deposits and withdrawals using payment methods that are convenient for you, and what fees are involved in doing so?

Once you have chosen a suitable and well-regulated broker for your needs, you then need to open up a margin account with them. This can typically be done by sending a check or with a bank wire transfer. Some online brokers will also take credit or debit card deposits, as well as electronic payments. The specific electronic payment companies accepted by brokers can differ widely, so be sure to check that your preferred payment service is supported if that matters to you.

Pricing Mechanics of Trading Commodities

Now that you have obtained a general sense for what you will need to learn on your way to becoming a successful commodity trader, and understand how to select an appropriate broker, you can start picking up some of the specific details and mechanics you will need to know to get started trading commodities that are discussed in the following sections of this chapter.

One of the most important things to understand about commodities trading is pricing and how prices are quotes. The next sections will discuss the process of obtaining real-time and dealing commodity prices, and how they are typically quoted by brokers.

Commodity Prices

Just about anyone new to trading commodities can easily learn to understand commodity prices. Obtaining a commodity quote usually involves getting the price per futures contract, which is also generally the published price.

The price per contract will give the trader the underlying commodity's price, which then must be multiplied by the amount of units of the underlying commodity to give an actual dollar amount of the contract. For example, if silver is trading at $15.00 an ounce, and its futures contract is for 5,000 troy ounces, the dollar amount for the transaction would be $75,000.

While the total dollar amount of this contract would be $75,000, many traders use a margin account to trade futures which gives them the opportunity to leverage their money considerably. For illustration purposes, assume that the trader is only required to post a 20% margin on futures trades.

The trader would then just need to deposit $15,000 of the original $75,000 trade in order to hold the silver futures position. They would also need to put up any brokerage or clearing fees the trader might incur, in addition to the $15,000 margin.

Two-Sided Commodity Prices

When asking for prices in the commodities futures markets, commodity prices will generally consist of two-sided markets that have both a bid and an offer price. Nevertheless, only the last sale price is typically available to the general public, and prices from the commodities exchange floor can often be delayed by as much as ten minutes.

While this might apply to the general public, an account holder with a commodities broker will typically have access to real-time commodity prices. They can obtain them either through an online trading platform or through telephone access to a commodities broker or a customer service representative at the brokerage.

Nevertheless, most exchange-traded commodities markets will still only offer the last sale price on a commodity, omitting the bid and offer market prices, regardless of whether the quote is made in real-time or not. The reason for this is that trading rings or "pits" generally get quite hectic with a large number of traders regularly buying and selling.

The commodities traders on the exchange floor generally only report the last traded price. This quote is then published, and a two-sided market can only be determined by a clerk or trader with visual access to the commodity trading pit. Nevertheless, getting commodity prices can still be achieved by phoning the commodities broker.

Obtaining Dealing Prices

When asking for commodity prices using a broker on the telephone, the process generally goes something like this: the trader phones up the broker and asks the broker what price the September crude oil contract is trading for. The broker will then look at their quote screen or computer and relay the last sale price.

The trader may have called because they have an interest in initiating a position. If so, they would then ask the broker to get a bid/offer quote on September crude oil. The broker then phones a clerk on the NYMEX exchange floor who can see the pit from their clerk's booth on the floor.

Floor brokers in the pit typically have "point clerks" which flash the bid/offer of the commodity to the phone clerks by using hand signals. The phone clerk can then relay that information to the broker who then tells their client.

Once the trader has gotten the commodity prices on the contracts they are interested in trading, the trader can then give an order to their broker to buy or sell at the prices quoted from the pit. Alternatively, they can give the broker an order away from the market that the broker can work on filling during the trading session.

To an outsider, the commodities trading floor may seem like pandemonium. Nevertheless, even during the most hectic and fast markets, order prevails to a considerable degree. As a result, commodity prices are set in an orderly fashion thereby allowing billions of dollars to safely change hands every day on the world's commodity exchanges.

Commodity Price Quotes

Most novice traders can readily understand commodity price quotes. The first consideration when reading a commodity quote involves the price per contract, which is also generally the published price.

The price per contract will give the trader the underlying commodity's price which then must be multiplied by the amount of units of the underlying commodity to give an actual dollar amount. For example, if gold is trading at $1000.00 an ounce, and the contract is for 100 troy ounces, the dollar amount for the transaction would be $100,000.

While the total dollar amount would be $100,000, many traders use margin accounts to trade futures which give them the opportunity to leverage their money. For illustration purposes, assume that the trader is required to post a 20% margin on futures trades.

The trader would then need to deposit $20,000 of the original $100,000 trade in order to hold the futures position. They would also need to put up any brokerage or clearing fees the trader might incur, in addition to the $20,000.

The rest of this section discusses the process for obtaining real-time quotes for commodities like gold, and it covers how to read commodity quotes.

Bid and Offer Spreads

In the commodities futures markets, commodity quotes generally consist of two-sided markets that have a bid and an offer price. Nevertheless, only the last sale price is typically available to the general public, and prices from the commodities exchange floor can often be delayed by as much as ten minutes.

While this may be the case for the general public, an account holder with a commodities broker will typically have access to real-time quotes. They can obtain them either through an online trading platform or through telephone access to a commodities broker or a customer service representative at the brokerage.

Nevertheless, most exchange-traded commodities markets will still only offer the last sale price on a commodity, omitting the bid and offer market prices, regardless of whether the quote is made in real-time or not. The reason for this is that trading rings or "pits" generally get quite hectic with a large number of traders regularly buying and selling.

The commodities traders on the exchange floor generally only report the last traded price. This quote is then published, and a two-sided market can only be determined by a clerk or trader with visual access to the commodity trading pit. Nevertheless, getting commodity quotes can still be achieved by phoning the commodities broker.

Getting Commodity Quotes Over the Phone

A typical request for commodity quotes through a broker over the phone usually goes something like this: the trader phones up the broker and asks the broker what price the September crude oil contract is trading for. The broker will then look at their quote screen or computer and relay the last sale price.

The trader may have an interest in initiating a position, so they would ask the broker to get the bid/offer quotes on September crude oil. The broker then phones a clerk on the NYMEX exchange floor who can see the pit from their clerk's booth on the floor.

Floor brokers in the pit typically have "point clerks" which flash the bid/offer of the commodity to the phone clerks by using hand signals. The phone clerk can then relay that information to the broker who then tells their client.

Once the trader has gotten commodity quotes on the contracts they are interested in trading, the trader can then give an order to their broker to buy or sell at the prices quoted from the pit. Alternatively, they can give the broker an order away from the market that the broker can work on filling during the trading session.

While the commodities trading floor may seem like pandemonium to an outsider, even during the most hectic and fast markets, order prevails to a large degree. This is the reason billions of dollars safely change hands every day in the exchange-traded commodities markets.

Entering Commodity Orders

Once you have developed the confidence to become a commodity trader after doing your homework in researching the relevant market, developing a trade plan and then trading it in a demo account for some time to assess its suitability and profitability, you will next need to take the plunge and start trading.

Naturally, the first step in doing so will be to open a live margin trading account with a reputable futures or online broker and have deposited the funds ready to use as margin for the transactions you want to make. Next, you will need to know how entering commodity orders works.

The main types of orders used in the commodity market are:

- **Market Orders**

    A market order is an order to buy or sell a futures contract or CFD on a commodity "at the market" or "at best." This means the broker you are dealing through should execute your order at the best price obtainable in the market. Usually this will be on the offer side of the market if the customer is buying or on the bid side of the market when they are selling, although this can vary depending on the size of the transaction.

    Nevertheless, take note that a market order never guarantees a price, but only that the broker will immediately execute the order. This becomes an important consideration in fast and volatile markets, or when dealing in especially large amounts, since the price an entire order is executed at may not be what is showing on a screen or trading platform at the time.

- **Limit Orders**

    A limit order is an order to buy or sell a futures contract or CFD at a "limit" price, which is specified with the order. The order will be filled if and only if the market goes to the limit price and stays there long enough for full execution. Accordingly, you run the risk of the order failing to be filled even if the price trades.

If the limit order is a buy order, the market price must be offered at the price specified in the order in sufficient amount for execution to be guaranteed. If it is a sell order, the market must be sufficiently bid at the price specified. Limit orders are extremely useful to technical traders that have pre-determined entry and exit points dictated by their trade plans.

Alternatively, limit orders can also be used to liquidate positions. Perhaps a trader holding a long position has the idea that the market will rise to reach a certain price in order to allow them liquidate their existing position at a profit. In this case, the trader can enter a limit order to sell their position at that better-than-market price in order to close out the transaction.

- **Stop Orders**

    A stop order is an order that gets activated when a certain price trades and then becomes a market order to allow the full completion of the transaction.

    A stop order is usually used to protectively liquidate a position, in which case they are often called stop-loss orders. Stops can also be used to initiate positions by trading "breakouts" in price action where technical factors have confirmed an upside or downside market bias.

    Furthermore, stop orders can be either a buy-stops or sell-stops. A buy-stop instructs the broker or dealing desk to buy at the market once the order price, which is higher than the current price, has traded. The execution of this stop order will limit losses if one is short the commodity, or will establish a long position, depending on the trader's initial intention.

    Conversely, a sell-stop will liquidate an existing long position or will initiate a short position once the specified price, which is lower than the prevailing market, has traded.

- **OCO or a One-Cancels-the-Other Order**

This type of order is especially popular with personal speculators trading their own account using technical analysis techniques. An OCO order usually consists of two separate orders to liquidate an existing position, along with a cancellation request for the remaining order if either order is executed.

Typically, one is a stop-loss order to protect the trading position against possible adverse price movements, while the other is a limit order to take profits on the trading position. If either order is filled, the other order is automatically canceled by the broker or dealing desk.

Commodity Forward and Futures Settlements

One of the more important aspects of trading commodities is settlement and delivery of physical commodities. Commodity producers like mining and agricultural companies may wish to deliver the physical commodity into a contract as specified, while industrial users may wish to accept physical delivery.

In contrast, most speculators will not want to deal with the hassle of delivery at all. As a result, they generally elect to close out contracts before delivery, roll them out to a later delivery date as the contracts approach delivery, or opt for cash settlement of the contract, if available.

Commodity futures contracts are similar to forward contracts in that a specific date for delivery of the commodity is chosen by the contracting parties. With commodity futures, however, the date chosen is uniform and pre-determined for all contracts of the particular commodity traded on the exchange for that delivery month.

On the other hand, commodity forwards are custom contracts entered into between two parties that agree upon a specific date, amount and price for future delivery.

The rest of this section explains the settlement procedure for commodity forwards and futures contracts and how futures contract settlements differ from forward contract settlements.

Commodity Forward Contracts and Settlement

Commodity forward contracts can be defined as non-standardized agreements between a buying party and a selling party to transact a specified amount of a commodity at some pre-determined future date at a specific price. The price of the commodity agreed upon at the time of entering into the contract is commonly known as the forward price.

Such forward contracts are typically entered into on the basis of credit lines, without margin or partial settlements being required, although they might involve some sort of collateralization during the term of the contract.

Furthermore, such forwards generally involve settling the contract for the agreed upon price on the delivery date. Because forwards are transacted in the Over-The-Counter or OTC market, they are not defined on regular standardized commodities, and can instead be customized to include a particular type or quality of shipment.

Forward contracts in commodities generally contain default clauses which require the defaulting party to reimburse the non-defaulting party for any losses incurred in the transaction. Defaults include either the buyer not being able to take delivery, or the seller not being able to deliver the commodity.

Settlement for a forward commodities contract is otherwise simply a matter of the contracting parties agreeing to deliver the commodity and to pay the agreed-upon price for the commodity upon its delivery.

Commodities Futures Contracts and Settlements

Commodity futures contracts differ in important ways from forward contracts in that they consist of standardized contracts on commodities of a minimum quality specification that are traded and cleared by a commodities exchange in standardized amounts for specific delivery dates.

Furthermore, delivery of the commodity into a futures contract is done at the option of the seller of the futures contract. They also need to notice the buyer that they intend to deliver the commodity physically into the futures contract.

The buyer cannot request delivery, but can elect to hold the contract until receiving notice from the seller if they intend to make delivery of the commodity.

Commodity Futures Contract Delivery Terms

The exchange where the commodities contract originates typically dictates which type of delivery notice will be used and the schedule for delivery. Notices are either transferable or non-transferable.

Transferable notices can allow a buyer to transfer their futures contract to another party prior to delivery, but if a seller notices a buyer with a non-transferable delivery notice, they cannot sell their futures contract notice on the floor of the exchange and must take delivery.

If the delivery is noticed before the last trading day in the contract, the trader can sell another futures contract against the commodity they received, although they can still incur costs associated with a non-transferable delivery.

A buyer with a transferable notice, on the other hand, is able to sell the delivery notice and offset the trade on the floor of the exchange to avoid physical delivery.

Notice and Last Trading Days for Futures Contracts

The commodities exchange also sets a day designated as the First Notice Day which is the first day a seller may notice a buyer of delivery, and is usually three business days before the first business day of the delivery month.

The exchange also sets a Last Notice Day which is the last day of the delivery period that the seller can notify a buyer of delivery. Typically, the last notice day will be two to seven business days before the last business day of the delivery month.

The last trading day of a futures contract varies from commodity to commodity. Nevertheless, the last trading day marks the day all outstanding futures contracts must be settled.

Commodity Trading Platforms

Commodities traders have traded futures electronically since the early 1990's when the Chicago Mercantile Exchange started the Globex electronic trading platform and later developed another platform for both trading and clearing futures electronically called ClearPort.

With the rise of online trading via the Internet over the past couple of decades, a commodities system now generally refers to the computer software which people use to execute commodity trades, which is also commonly known as a trading platform.

The rest of this section discusses topics relating to commodities trading platform software, and how many forex and CFD brokers offer basic commodity trading from their platforms.

Commodity Trading Platforms

What is a trading platform? Basically, a trading platform refers to software from which a trader can get quotes, enter trades, research commodities, draw charts, perform technical analysis, read news and obtain other pertinent information on a commodity. In some cases, traders can even run an automated trading system on such a platform.

Most, if not all online brokers provide a trading platform to support their client's trading or support access via a popular third party trading platform like MetaTrader. Such trading platforms can be very simple, with only trade entry and quote capabilities like might be seen on a mobile phone trading platform. They can also be very elaborate, with the possibility of researching fundamentals, weather activity, charts, news, trade signals and other useful features for traders.

Online brokers typically offer a free trading platform to traders when opening an account, and they might offer extra features such as high-quality financial news wires like Reuters for more active traders and social trading. Nevertheless, in the vast majority of cases, a trading platform is only as good for making profits as the trader using it.

A variety of trading platforms are available which are well-worth checking out. Some online brokers will even allow you to practice using their trading platform before opening a funded account using a demo account funded with virtual money. Furthermore, some trading platforms now allow traders to input their trading systems via computer coding languages in order to fully or partially automate their trading activities.

Trading Platform Features

While trading platforms often vary among different online brokerages, they all share some basic features. These features include:

- **Secure Online Log-in** – just about all online brokers share this feature and those with premium accounts can often log in to V.I.P. areas not available to other less-affluent customers.

- **Market Watch Page** – online brokers will usually have an Internet page where you can monitor the prices of those you choose among many different commodities, as well as forex currency pairs, cryptocurrencies like Bitcoin, stocks and stock indexes. This price information will often include the bids and offers, trading volume figures, and general market indicators.

- **News and Information Page** – almost all trading platforms offered by online brokers offer an informational news feed, either from Reuters or from some other business news wire service like AP Dow Jones.

- **Order Entry Page** – once you have funded an account with a broker and have securely logged in, you can then go to the order entry page. This is where you will be buying and selling commodity CFDs over the Internet. The order entry page will give the current bid and offer for the CFD in the market before you enter the order. In addition, you will be asked to confirm if you really want to execute the trade.

- **Confirmation Page** – once you have entered an order for a CFD, you will then receive a confirmation if the order is executed. This will usually alert you with a pop-up window which will then take you to a trade confirmation page.

Automated Commodity Trading

In addition to the trading platforms discussed in the previous section, another type of commodity trading system rely on programmed algorithmic models to generate trading signals or even execute deals. Commodity system trading of that type originated in the 1980's with the first PC's and was until recently the exclusive domain of professional commodities traders.

Automated or algorithmic commodity trading has been implemented for decades by professional trading firms, primarily to trade and arbitrage assets against derivative products such as stock indexes and futures contracts. Nevertheless, it was not until online trading accounts were made available that the general public has been able to take advantage of automated trading. To implement this, a trading platform provided by a trading software developer is often used in tandem with an online broker's deal execution capability.

Automatic trading software and signal generators are currently widely available for the forex market, where a wide variety of software is used for the generation of trading signals. Even completely-automated forex trading robots have become increasingly popular lately with online traders. Some forex trading platforms and brokers also permit the execution of popular trading commodities like gold, silver and oil.

Although the forex and CFD market has the lion's share of automated trading software available to retail accounts, several online trading software companies now offer automated commodity trading packages.

While automated commodity trading has not yet been developed to the point that forex trading robot software has when it comes to being available to the general public, a number of other options for commodity traders are currently available when trading CFDs online.

Automated Trading Systems

An algorithmic commodity trading system need not be fully automated, and they can either be purchased online or developed by anyone that knows what to look for in a commodity market to signal a trade. The key to developing a successful trading system for commodities involves first knowing which commodities to trade and then how to trade them profitably.

Selecting the right commodity depends primarily on what type of trading system will be used, as will be discussed in a subsequent chapter of this book. For example, a system can be developed for day trading, in which case the parameters of the system must require that all trades be liquidated at the end of the trading day.

Other trading systems might involve a longer-term outlook on the commodities selected. These might incorporate swing trading and range trading strategies, or even longer-term trading strategies such as trend trading.

Regardless of what trading system a trader decides upon, position-sizing and other money-management techniques incorporated into the trading plan can increase the profitability of the trading system considerably. As a result, these elements should not be overlooked when developing a commodity trading system, so be sure to review the subsequent chapters containing that information.

Trading Signal Generators

One of the most popular types of trading software currently being widely used for the forex, commodity and stock markets involves signal generation. Signal generators operate based on certain trading parameters. For example, they might examine price movements over time, coupled with other technical indicators such as moving averages. The system would then use objective and pre-determined criteria to generate buy or sell signals on a currency pair, stock or commodity futures contract.

While widely-used in the forex market, signal-generating software for commodities has not enjoyed the same popularity as the analogous forex software currently on the market. In theory, signal generators should work for commodities systems just as well as for the forex market since many of the parameters and techniques used are not specific to the trading vehicle.

Nevertheless, the spreads, commissions and execution capability may differ significantly between markets. Still, a number of forex trading software packages allow the purchaser to use them for trading gold, silver and crude oil futures.

Dedicated Commodities Systems Software

While the forex market maintains perhaps the largest variety of online electronic trading software, several companies offer commodities futures trading software. Automated trading software for commodities has not yet been made readily available to the public, despite being widely available in the forex market and sometimes to those trading CFDs.

Nevertheless, several commodities futures trading platforms can be accessed. Although they are usually not automated, except in the generation of trading signals, traders must still input their own orders and execute their own trades.

Furthermore, the electronic trading services currently available to commodities futures traders are usually offered on a subscription basis. In some cases they can be obtained for free, depending on the amount of transactions the trader makes on the electronic trading platform. Otherwise, the service is offered for a monthly fee that can range from $49 to $249, depending on the amount and size of futures transactions executed.

Unfortunately, fully automated commodities systems trading software has a long way to go in order to catch up to the level which the forex market has attained in automated software packages currently available to the public.

Nevertheless, as an increasing number of people become interested in trading commodities electronically, more software that is currently only accessible to commodities trading professionals will be made available to retail traders.

Commodity Trading Tips

For most people, getting started as a speculative commodity trader involves getting some sound advice from experts about what to do and what to avoid when trading.

Fortunately, the financial markets have matured to the point where a general consensus has emerged about the elements necessary for being consistently successful as a trader.

What follows are five top trading tips for anyone serious about trading profitably in the financial markets over the long term:

1. **Get a Good Trading Education**

Certainly, reading this book and others written by professional commodity traders will be a great initial step to give you an edge as you start out trading. In addition, you will want to start dedicating a certain amount of time each week to educating yourself on how to execute commodity trades, how to keep records, and other aspects of trading that are fundamental to your future success.

Novice traders should also study what fundamental information other commodity traders are watching in the market to give them a better idea of what news affects the commodity market and why it does so. Also, remember to develop a good understanding of technical analysis since it can really help you develop a trade plan. Both of those key analysis topics will be discussed in further detail in Chapter 7 of this book.

A number of useful resources for learning can be found by searching online, as well as complete online trading courses. Furthermore, you can participate in online forums and Facebook groups in order to ask questions and get answers from other commodity traders with similar interests to yours. Nevertheless, no substitute exists for getting mentored by a professional trader who can guide you personally as you progress toward developing your own expertise.

2. Plan Your Trades

Once you have obtained a sufficient amount of education about the commodity market you are interested in trading and have familiarized yourself about the key technical and fundamental indicators relevant to the market, you can begin to develop a trading system or trade plan. A good trading system will advise you objectively of the optimum prices and times to initiate and liquidate trading positions.

Along with a reasonable risk management plan, a topic that will be discussed further in Chapter 8 of this book, you are practically ready to trade once you have come up with a good trade plan that is both consistently profitable and suitable for your lifestyle.

Alternatively, if you are going to be trading CFDs, your trade plan can involve creating or purchasing a trading robot that will automatically enter and liquidate commodity trades for you. Nevertheless, please be advised that many such robots on the market have a hard time living up to their historical profitability in live trading.

3. Trade Your Plan

After you have developed a coherent trading plan that fits your needs, lifestyle and personality, be firmly committed to sticking to your trading rules in a disciplined way. Basically, humans can all be victims of their own psychology and get emotionally involved while trading, which can thereby result in costly mistakes.

Typical trading discipline errors include: getting too greedy when taking a profit; doubling up on losing trades instead of cutting losses; and letting winning trades turn into losers. If you do make mistakes, make sure you learn from them by keeping a detailed trading journal and analyzing it periodically.

4. Pick Trades With a High Probability of Success

Your trading system should have an optimal risk/reward ratio as part of its criteria for each and every trade recommended. Your chances of success as a trader over the long term can be much better when carefully selecting trades with a high probability of success.

For example, you can aim for trades with an estimated risk/reward ratio of 1 to 2 or 1:2, which would mean that you plan on risking one unit to make two units.

5. Manage Your Money and Risks Appropriately

Money management has consistently proven itself to be crucial to successful trading over the long term and will be discussed in detail in Chapter 6 of this book, along with the related topic of risk management.

Furthermore, one of the most important things to learn when trading is to avoid over-extending your trading account by taking more risk than is appropriate for the amount of money you are trading with. In general, good money management practices include limiting your losses with stop-loss orders and allowing your profits to run by using trailing stops, which can also improve your risk/reward ratio.

Basically, doing your homework before you start trading can save you both money and emotional turmoil. It can also give you the confidence you need to become truly successful at trading. Hopefully, following these commodity trading tips will also help you improve your trading experience over time even if you lose some money initially.

CHAPTER 4: POPULAR COMMODITIES TO TRADE

When you are starting up your trading business, you will probably want to decide what commodity markets you wish to follow and trade in. If you are a producer or industrial user of commodities, then your trading vehicles will largely be determined by your hedging needs.

If you are speculating, then you can trade virtually any commodity market you can execute a transaction in, although more liquid and moderately volatile commodity markets tend to suit most trading strategies best.

The rest of this chapter will cover some of the more popular commodities traders often choose to speculate in.

Precious and Base Metals

Precious metals are rare and naturally occurring metallic elements with considerable economic value that are often resistant to corrosion in air. While precious metals like gold and silver had a history as currencies in their own right or as standards by which paper currencies were valued, they are now mostly used as investments and as industrial commodities.

Gold, silver, platinum, and palladium are the generally recognized precious metals that traders can trade futures and CFDs on, and each of them has a unique ISO 4217 currency code, giving them further status as currencies that are not associated with a particular nation or economy.

Although the precious metals each have notable industrial applications, those less rare or non-precious metals that are also commonly called "base" or minor metals also have futures markets traders can operate in, most notably on the London Metals Exchange or LME where the traditional open outcry method of price discovery is still in use, although most transactions now take place electronically.

These base metals include copper, iron, tin, aluminum, lead, nickel, steel, cobalt and molybdenum. Metallic alloys used in industrial applications, such as steel and aluminum alloys, also have associated futures contracts that can be traded.

The following sections will describe some of the most popular precious and base metals that have sufficiently liquid futures markets to trade and for which CFDs are available for those retail traders with less risk capital.

Gold

Trading gold has occupied man since pre-history. The precious metal has been used since the beginning of recorded history for a variety of uses, such as in the making of jewelry and coin. It is also often considered a safe haven investment in times of geopolitical turmoil and social unrest.

Gold has also been traditionally used by investors as storage of value and inflation hedge, and gold standards have often been used as the basis to support the use of fiat currency monetary policies, such as in the post WWII Bretton Woods system of fixed exchange rates that fixed the price of gold in U.S. Dollar terms and then pegged other fiat currencies to the Dollar at fixed exchange rates.

As part of its attraction, gold is also among the most malleable pure metals known and is resistant against oxidation from air or water. As a result, it is used in many high-tech industrial applications, such as in electronics and wiring, because of its impressive conductivity and resistance to corrosion.

Because of gold's traditional storage of value role and multiple other uses, trading in the precious metal has been popular for millennia. The most prevalent form of gold trading for investors, hedgers and speculators currently occurs in the futures market where gold remains one of the most liquid commodities traded.

Futures on gold allows for additional leverage and the benefit of a large number of speculators that keep the market liquid. In addition, gold futures are traded on regulated exchanges and make trading gold relatively easy for anyone with enough funds to trade futures. For smaller traders, CFD trading of gold via online brokers is also becoming increasingly popular

Gold as an Inflation Hedge

While gold has traditionally been known as an inflation hedge, many other investments have returned as much or more than gold. A case in point is that one U.S. Dollar worth of gold in 1801 is now worth $1.39 while the $1 is now worth less than $0.07.

Nevertheless, trading gold has increased in popularity due to how the metal is perceived, its value in the manufacture of jewelry and in high-tech applications and because it can theoretically be used as money.

Although many people believe that gold is an inflation hedge, the period between 1980 and 1999 saw the price of gold decline by a factor of 3 with the price of gold dropping from almost $800 to under $250 with inflation occurring during the entire period.

The price of gold is more influenced by a perception of quality in investments and the flight to a "safe-haven" during periods of uncertainty as can be witnessed when world political instability impacts the price of gold favorably.

When the value of paper money declines the price of gold generally reacts inversely while still holding its value during inflationary cycles because gold is a tangible solid asset unlike a currency.

Where Gold Trades

Gold trading is worldwide for both the spot and exchange traded futures market. The following lists the main centers for worldwide gold trading:
- The London Gold Market
- The Chinese Gold and Silver Exchange in Hong Kong
- The COMEX division of the New York Mercantile Exchange or NYMEX
- The Tokyo Commodities Exchange or TOCOM in Japan
- The Chicago Board of Trade or CBOT
- The Istanbul Gold Exchange and the Shanghai Gold Exchange

The most popular vehicle for trading gold is the COMEX exchange's futures contract for 100 Troy ounces. Nevertheless, two smaller contracts have increased in popularity: the E-mini Gold contract for 33 ounces and the miNY Gold contract for 50 ounces both traded electronically on the CME Group's Globex electronic trading platform.

India Gold Trading

India has relatively recently begun trading in gold futures with trading in Gold Guineas. The Gold Guinea refers to the first machine-minted gold coin in Great Britain minted between 1663 and 1813. Futures on this form of gold are traded on India's National Multi-Commodity Exchange or NMCE and are for 8 grams of gold coins with a fineness of 0.999 and are quoted in Indian Rupees.

Silver

Trading silver CFDs and futures has traditionally afforded investors and speculators both a hedging and speculative opportunity. Producers or processors use these futures contracts for commercial hedging purposes as a way to manage their risk resulting from anticipated purchases or sales of the precious metal. Speculators can also participate in the silver market and can start trading silver futures without having any physical silver.

Silver has traditionally been used in the production of coins, utensils, jewelry and photography. Silver is also a traditional way for people to store wealth, in part because silver has often been acquired to hedge against inflation risk. The price of silver, while only a fraction of the price of gold, has traditionally followed gold closely since similar economic conditions affect them both because of their role as mediums for the storage of wealth.

Unlike gold, silver has a number of industrial uses which can make the metal's price extremely volatile. The price of silver reached a recent low of $3.92 in 1992, and the metal is currently trading between $16 and $17 an ounce, to provide an idea of the wide price range this precious metal can exhibit.

While trading silver futures happens on a global basis, a number of principal exchanges and electronic trading platforms serve as the main futures markets for silver. The rest of this section covers silver futures trading and principle silver futures markets and contract specifications for trading silver.

Principal Silver Futures Exchanges

Trading silver futures has traditionally taken place at the COMEX, originally the Commodities Exchange, in New York City. The COMEX became part of the New York Mercantile Exchange or NYMEX in 1994, and the NYMEX was later bought by the CME Group, formerly the Chicago Mercantile Exchange, in 2008. While the COMEX and NYMEX are owned by the CME group, COMEX silver futures contracts are still listed as though the COMEX was a separate exchange.

All U.S. Silver futures are quoted in U.S. Dollars. The full-size COMEX silver futures contract is for 5,000 troy ounces of silver, with a minimum fluctuation of $.005 an ounce or $25 per contract. The trading symbol for standard silver futures contracts is SI.

Other Silver Futures

In addition to traditional silver futures, two smaller futures contracts offered to the public have become a popular way for trading silver, especially for smaller speculators. These are:

- **E-mini Silver** – the E-mini contract is traded on the CME Group's Globex and ClearPort electronic trading platforms around the clock from Sunday night through to Friday afternoon. The contracts are regulated by the COMEX and are for 1,000 troy ounces of silver with a minimum fluctuation of $0.0125 an ounce or $12.50 per contract. Trading symbol for the E-mini Silver future is XSN.

- **miNY Silver** – these futures are traded electronically on the Chicago Mercantile Exchange's Globex electronic trading platform. miNY Silver contracts are for 2,500 troy ounces of silver with a minimum fluctuation of $0.0125 or $31.25 per contract. The trading symbol for miNY Silver is QI.

India Silver Futures

In addition to the U.S. Silver futures, an active market for trading silver futures exists in India, which has an active market on the Multi-Commodities Exchange or MCX based in Mumbai. Prices are quoted in Indian Rupees and contracts are for 1 Kilogram of Silver each.

Silver accounts for a large part of bullion traded and shows rising demand as recent economic conditions justify rising prices for silver, gold and other strategic metals. Any investor with an interest in hedging against inflation risk could consider adding silver or some other precious metal to their portfolio.

Platinum

Platinum refer to a malleable, dense, ductile metallic substance considered a precious metal. Much like gold, platinum is a commodity that has importance in the manufacture of jewelry. Unlike gold, however, platinum has various industrial uses, thereby making the metal both a strategic and precious metal.

Although platinum was known for many years by pre-Columbian Native Americans, the element was first found by Spaniards in Columbian mines in Central America who named it *platina*, or little silver. It was also mentioned in 1557 by Italian Julius Caesar Scaliger. The Spanish found the metal impossible to melt and so considered it an unwanted impurity in their silver mining process.

Because of its unique chemical properties, other primary uses of platinum have to do with petroleum refining and the manufacture of catalytic converters for automotive pollution control systems and oxygen sensors as well as in electrical contacts, electrodes and laboratory equipment. In fact, about two-thirds of the worldwide production of platinum currently goes towards the manufacture of automotive catalytic converters, with the balance of production being used for jewelry and other applications.

The rest of this section covers what platinum is, its uses, occurrence in nature and production process, as well as its principal commodities futures markets.

Where Platinum is Mined

Despite it being a naturally-occurring metal, finding platinum can be extremely challenging. Scientists estimate that the metal occurs at a concentration of only 0.003 ppb in the Earth's surface crust. Also, native platinum occurs only in very few places on the planet and can be found mostly combined with iridium in a compound known as platiniridium.

Otherwise, platinum can be found in alluvial deposits combined with other minerals and also as a sulfide in copper and nickel deposits. A major source of platinum derived this way occurs in the Sudbury basin of Ontario, Canada.

Other important locations where platinum occurs naturally include the Bushveld Complex in South Africa and in the large nickel and copper deposits near the town of Norilsk in Russia.

South Africa accounts for the lion's share of production, with 80% of world production originating in that country. Russia is second and Canada third in terms of global production of this highly-prized commodity. The United States possesses a smaller reserve of the metal in the Absaroka Range in Montana.

Platinum Production

Platinum generally needs an extraction process to result in a commercially acceptable product. The process begins with the end product of the electro-refining of copper. A substance called "anode mud" remains after the electro-refining process, at which point the extraction of platinum and other metals of the platinum group ensues.

If the presence of platinum is detected, extraction can commence by floating other impurities out since platinum is extremely heavy. In addition, platinum has no magnetic properties, unlike iron or nickel which can be extracted magnetically.

Trading Platinum

Platinum trading has grown considerably in the last 20 years as emission controls for automobiles have become a matter of law in many of the United States. The main platinum futures trading center is the New York Mercantile Exchange or NYMEX, in addition to the Chicago Mercantile Exchange's Globex and ClearPort electronic trading platforms.

The full futures contract size on those exchanges is for 50 troy ounces, with futures prices quoted in U.S. Dollars. The minimum fluctuation is of $0.10 per troy ounce or $5.00 per contract. Platinum futures are traded under the symbol PL. The NYMEX also offers an E- mini contract of 500 grams per contract. In addition, Platinum futures also trade on the Tokyo Commodities Exchange and the Multi-Commodities Exchange in India.

Palladium

Palladium refers to a tarnish-resistant metallic element with a silvery-white appearance that can be found in a variety of ores like platinum, gold and copper. Because of its industrial uses, palladium falls into the categories of both a precious and an industrial metal.

The rest of this section covers the definition, role and production of palladium as an industrial and precious metal, as well as how palladium trades.

Palladium as a Commodity and Industrial Metal

As a commodity, palladium's International Organization for Standardization or ISO 4217 code is XPD. This code, also known as a currency code that identifies different currencies and precious metals, distinguishes palladium as one of only four metals to have such a code. The other metals consist of gold, silver and platinum.

Palladium has a wide variety of industrial uses that includes the manufacture of components for automotive emissions systems such as catalytic converters. The metal also has a place in the manufacture of jewelry, electrical contacts, spark plugs for aircraft and blood sugar test strips, among other uses.

Palladium Production

Palladium occurs naturally and can be found as a free metal alloyed with other metals of the platinum group source metals such as gold and silver. The metal typically requires many metric tons of ore to be mined and processed to obtain just a small amount of palladium.

Nickel and copper deposits also yield a small amount of palladium, but this generally requires an extraction process to obtain a commercially-acceptable palladium product. The process begins with the end product of the electro-refining of copper. A substance called "anode mud" remains after the electro-refining, at which point the extraction of palladium and other metals of the platinum group ensues.

Russia was the largest producer of palladium in 2005, accounting for over 50% of world production. South Africa, Canada and the United States followed, with other notable deposits occurring in Australia, Ethiopia and South America. The largest single known source for palladium is the Norilsk-Talnakh nickel deposits in Russia, followed by the Bushveld Igneous Complex of South Africa and the Lac des Îles igneous complex in Ontario, Canada.

Palladium Trading

Palladium, while not as highly-priced as gold or platinum, can and will track both other precious metals relatively closely. Nevertheless, because of its similarity to platinum both in its origin and extraction process, the metal tends to track platinum more closely.

Spot palladium prices are fixed on the London Platinum and Palladium Market or LPPM. The market publishes daily price fixings for both metals, much like the London Bullion Market which fixes gold prices.

The prices for both metals are fixed twice per day by four members of the LPPM which agree on a fair bid price. Prices for the two metals are expressed in U.S. Dollars and represent what LPPM members are willing to pay for the metals at the time of the fixing. All trades are for cash and involve delivery of the physical commodity, with settlement taking place within two days.

Palladium futures trade on the New York Mercantile Exchange or NYMEX, as well as on the CME Group's Globex and ClearPort electronic trading platforms. The contract size for these futures is for 100 troy ounces of Palladium per contract.

Futures contracts are quoted in U.S. Dollars with a minimum fluctuation of $0.05 per troy ounce or $5.00 per contract. The symbol for Palladium futures is PA.

Copper

As a commodity, copper refers to a very malleable and ductile orange metal that has excellent electrical conductivity and heat-transmission properties. In addition, copper has seen thousands of years of use as a currency that continues to this day in the minting of coins like the copper one penny coin used in the United States.

Copper is also used in wiring where it serves as a very good conductor of electricity and the popular metal finds many uses that involve building wiring, as well as electrical applications like machines, electromagnets and integrated circuits. The metal is also used industrially in various metal alloys and as an efficient heat conductor in applications like cooking pans.

Copper has stayed relatively inexpensive because it has a wide distribution in the mineral content of the Earth's crust. Because of this and its many uses, copper has become a particularly actively-traded commodity among the base metals. The rest of this section covers copper as a commodity including what it is, where its futures trade and on what contract terms.

Copper Production

The majority of copper production comes from the extraction of copper ore from large open pit mines such as the Chuquicamata mine in Chile and the El Chino mine in New Mexico. Chile accounts for almost one-third of world copper production, followed by the United States, Indonesia and Peru.

Copper occurs naturally all over the planet and at current extraction rates would take 5 million years to deplete. Nevertheless, only a small fraction of copper reserves are viable to be extracted economically, and estimates of existing reserves vary between 25 and 60 years' worth of production.

For this reason, copper prices can be extremely volatile despite it being a recyclable metal. Copper reached a 60-year low in 1999 of $0.60 per pound and quintupled by 2006 when it reached $3.75 per pound.

By February of 2009, dwindling demand and a general softening of world commodity prices had impacted copper to drive its price down to 1.51 per pound. Currently, copper is trading in the $3.25 to $3.50 range

Copper Futures

While trading in copper futures now occurs on a global basis, a number of principal exchanges and electronic trading platforms currently serve as the main futures markets for copper as a commodity.

The main resource for trading copper futures is via the New York Mercantile Exchange or NYMEX's COMEX division. The popular orange metal is actively-traded on that exchange using the symbol HG.

Each futures contract for copper covers a trading amount of 25,000 pounds. This needs to consist of Grade 1 electrolytic copper that is approved by the exchange it trades on.

Copper futures prices traded on the COMEX will be quoted in U.S. Dollars. Also, the minimum price fluctuation for such copper futures is

$0.0005 per pound. This works out to $12.50 per futures contract.

The last trading day for the COMEX copper futures contract falls on the third to last business day for the maturing delivery month. Trading ends on that exchange for a copper futures contract once business closes for that final day.

Energy Commodities

Since humans walked out of the forests and into cities, energy has been an indispensable asset to improve human survival rates, increase the speed of transportation and drive industrial activity. Modern humans living in developed countries have become notably dependent on energy products to maintain their lifestyles, thereby making demand for energy-producing commodities quite consistent.

Traditional sources of energy that are obtained from fossil fuel deposits include crude oil, heating oil, ethanol, coal and gasoline. Nevertheless, the use of these substances is gradually giving way to cleaner and more renewable energy sources like solar, wind, geothermal, hydroelectric and tidal power.

Although rarely used for investment purposes, certain energy commodities have sufficiently active futures markets and price volatility to make them an interesting trading vehicle for speculators. Such traders will typically use futures contracts, options or CFDs to trade the energy commodity markets.

Futures, forwards and options on energy products can also be used by hedgers to protect against adverse price changes, whether they are producers concerned about energy price declines or industrial users concerned about energy price rises.

The following sections will describe in greater depth some of the most popular energy products that have sufficiently liquid futures markets to trade and for which CFDs are often available for those retail traders with less risk capital. Specifically, these are crude oil, heating oil and ethanol.

Crude Oil

In the world of commodities, the most geo-politically influenced operations involve trading oil futures. Crude oil has an importance in the world economy few other commodities share.

This section covers the nature of crude oil and the different benchmarks, its geo-political importance and principal trading markets.

What is Crude Oil?

Crude Oil, also referred to as petroleum consists of a dark flammable liquid which occurs in nature and made up of a complex mixture of hydrocarbons as well as other natural organic compounds. Crude oil reserves are located underground and the composition of each different type of oil varies depending on the drilling location. Crude oil can be either "heavy" or "light."

Light oil produces more gasoline because it has a low viscosity and is free-flowing at room temperature. In addition light oil has a higher concentration of light hydrocarbons than heavier oils. Sweet refers to oil which contains less than 0.05% sulfuric content, versus sour crude which contains more than 0.05% sulfur.

Sweet light oil trades at a premium because it requires less refining to meet sulfuric standards of consuming countries. It is wise to know what kind of oil you are trading before trading oil futures. Crude oil is divided into four different benchmarks:

- **OPEC Reference Basket** – a weighted average of different types of oil blends from several Organization of Oil Producing Countries (OPEC).

- **Brent Blend** – consists of oil from 15 different oil fields in the North Sea.

- **West Texas Intermediate** – a sweet and light oil of high quality.

- **Dubai** - Oman, a Middle Eastern sour crude oil benchmark.

Crude Oil Trading

The most active market for trading oil futures would be on the New York Mercantile Exchange or NYMEX. Standardized futures contracts for benchmark West Texas Intermediate Crude make up the most heavily traded commodities futures contracts on that exchange.

Futures contracts at the NYMEX trade for 30 consecutive months in 1,000 U.S. barrel units or 42,000 gallons each and are quoted in U.S. Dollars with a minimum fluctuation of $0.01 per barrel or $10 a contract.

Trading oil futures is also possible for Brent Crude oil. The contracts are primarily traded on the Intercontinental Exchange or ICE, but are also traded on the NYMEX. Brent Crude is also a light sweet crude oil and is a blend of oil from 15 different oil fields in the North Sea between Norway and Denmark. The contracts are also for 1,000 U.S. barrels and are quoted in U.S. Dollars.

Both types of crude oil futures contracts as well as an E-mini contract for Light Sweet Crude oil can be traded electronically on the CME Group's Globex electronic trading platform.

Risks of Trading Oil Futures

Because of leverage in the commodities futures business, typically only 20% of the futures contract value needs to be put up to hold a position. This may seem like a great deal, but only if you are right on the direction of the market.

If not, your 20% could disappear in a heartbeat in a volatile market like the crude oil market. Commodity markets in general carry a risk not generally recommended for a person looking for a secure investment. Know what you are getting into before you start trading and have a trading plan beforehand.

Heating Oil

The production of heating oil, also known as no. 2 fuel oil, takes up an estimated 25% of a barrel of oil. After gasoline production, heating oil accounts for the largest part of crude oil elaboration.

This section covers what heating oil is, how and where it is primarily consumed, and where heating oil futures trade.

What is Heating Oil?

Heating oil generally refers to a distillate fuel oil derived from petroleum and commonly used for household space heating. Heating oil makes up the main fuel source in the heating of over eight million of households in the United States.

Since the principal use for heating oil involves residential space heating, most of the U.S. domestic consumption of Heating Oil occurs between the months of October and March. This commodity can exhibit high volatility, not only because of the seasonal nature of its consumption, but also because it is a petroleum by-product and therefore directly affected by world oil prices.

Heating oil in the United States typically comes from two sources: imports from abroad and domestic oil refineries. In the refining of crude oil, both diesel fuel and heating oil come from what is known as the "distillate" fuel product family.

In the United States, imports of heating oil generally come from Canada and Venezuela, and the domestic resources for the distribution of heating oil include: pipelines, trucks, rail cars, tanker vehicles and barges.

Heating Oil Price Factors

The main influence on the price of heating oil involves the going price of a barrel of crude oil. Furthermore, seasonal factors in consumption, together with the limitations of how much refiners can produce to meet winter demand, make up the second largest influence on heating oil prices.

The limitations refineries have in producing more heating oil have to do with the seasonal nature of production and the fact that refineries would need to produce other petroleum products which might not be readily sold in the winter season in order to produce more heating oil.

Many refiners use the summer months to produce and stockpile heating oil in preparation for the cold season. In this way, refiners are able to meet the higher demand of the winter months.

Heating Oil Futures Trading

The main market for Heating Oil futures is on the New York Mercantile Exchange where contracts are traded on the exchange floor. In addition, the contracts are also traded on the Chicago Mercantile Exchange's Globex and Clearport electronic trading platforms.

The New York Harbor No. 2 Heating Oil futures contract is for 1,000 barrels or 42,000 gallons of heating oil and is traded under the symbol HO. Prices are quoted in U.S. Dollars and the minimum fluctuation is $0.0001 per gallon or $4.20 per contract.

In addition to the full NYMEX futures contract, an E-mini contract of half the size of the full futures contract can also be traded on the CME Group's Globex electronic trading platform. Nevertheless, settlement for the E-mini futures is financial, so no delivery can be taken on those contracts.

Ethanol

Ethanol is also known as ethyl alcohol, grain alcohol, drinking alcohol and pure alcohol. It consists of a flammable, volatile and colorless liquid that is generally obtained from the fermentation of grains and is best known as the psychoactive component in alcoholic beverages.

Besides being used around the world as an intoxicant, ethanol makes an excellent solvent and is used in products such as: medicines, flavorings, perfumes and other products intended for human consumption. It is also sometimes used in automobile fuel.

The rest of this section covers the definition, production and role of ethanol as an important fuel source, intoxicant and trading commodity.

Ethanol as a Fuel

Ethanol has become a popular fuel and fuel additive for automobiles and this makes up the largest single use of the commodity in today's economy. Even though Henry Ford's first mass-produced car, the Model T, was designed to run on ethanol, the use of ethanol as a motor fuel has only recently become widespread.

Furthermore, because of falling grain prices and rising oil prices, the idea of clean-burning ethanol as an alternative fuel has taken hold. In addition, the U.S. government offers gasoline refiners a tax incentive of 45 cents for every gallon of gasoline they blend with ethanol.

This subsidy, added to the low price of corn which had lost roughly half its value from over $7 to a bit over $3, has made adding ethanol to gasoline a means for refiners to save over $1 per gallon in production costs.

Ethanol Production

Ethanol production generally begins with a dry-milling step in which the commodity — usually corn, wheat, barley, sugar or beets— is ground in order to facilitate the processing. After grinding the commodity, all the sugar is released from the base plant and left for microbes to ferment, thereby producing ethanol and carbon dioxide in the process. Wet-milling can also be used to begin the ethanol production process.

The largest producers of ethanol in the world are Brazil and the United States, together accounting for 69% of global ethanol production in 2006. Brazil uses ethanol for automotive fuel, and more than 20% of Brazil's automobiles can run on pure ethanol fuel which can be obtained commercially in that country.

Brazil maintains their ethanol-dependent fleet of automobiles with a large industrial infrastructure designed for the elaboration of ethanol from the country's large sugar cane industry. Sugar cane contains 30% more sucrose, the sugar that forms the base source of ethanol, than corn.

The United States' production of ethanol largely comes from corn, with a nationwide production capacity of over seven billion gallons of ethanol per year. Legislation in the United States mandates growth in ethanol production to 7.5 billion gallons per year by 2012, and the ethanol industry's growth has expanded dramatically due to a combination of higher oil prices and the availability of cheap grains for fermentation.

Nevertheless, ethanol continues to be used more as an additive to gasoline, with a 10% blend commonly known as "gasohol." This blend is widely available in parts of the Midwestern United States.

Ethanol Futures Trading

Because the principal world market in corn is based at the Chicago Board of Trade or CBOT, ethanol futures also trade in this birthplace of modern futures trading. The CBOT futures trade under the symbol AG and cover 29,000 gallons of ethanol. Prices are quoted in U.S. Dollars and the minimum fluctuation is for one-tenth of one cent $0.0001 per gallon or $2.90 per contract.

Since the market for ethanol futures is relatively new, it tends to lack liquidity and so can trade rather thinly. Nevertheless, the contracts remain an effective hedging tool for the ethanol-production and processing industry.

Agricultural or Soft Commodities

Agricultural or soft commodities form the basis of the current food supply for humans and other animals, as well as providing natural fibers for clothing and other applications.

In the modern era, agricultural commodities are typically grown intensively by industrial concerns like large farms and plantations. They differ in their production method from hard commodities that are generally mined, like the precious and base metals.

Traditional agricultural commodities include plant-derived staples like coffee, cotton, sugar, corn and soybeans. They also include livestock, as well as the various body parts of slaughtered animals and other animal products like milk and eggs that can be obtained from living creatures.

Of course, human tastes can change, and this can affect the future levels of soft commodity prices. For example, as public awareness grows of the mistreatment of animals in intensive animal agricultural facilities and slaughterhouses, as well as the severe environmental and climate change impact of this industry, the use and killing of animals for human food is notably declining in popularity. As a result, considerable investment is now being made in "clean meat" products that either do not require animal products at all or are grown in a laboratory from animal cells.

Other factors that can affect demand for agricultural commodities include the perceived healthfulness of a particular food product relative to another. For example, many people are switching away from animal-derived products that often contain high levels of saturated fats to a more plant-based diet for health reasons, thereby reducing demand for meat, dairy and eggs, while increasing demand for high-protein legumes like soybeans.

Although rarely used for investment purposes, certain soft commodities have sufficiently active futures markets and price volatility to make them an interesting trading vehicle for speculators. Such traders will typically use futures contracts, options or CFDs to trade the various agricultural commodity markets.

Futures, forwards and options on agricultural products can also be used by hedgers to protect against adverse price changes, whether they are producers concerned about soft commodity price declines or industrial consumers concerned about price rises.

The following sections will describe in greater depth some of the most popular agricultural products that have sufficiently liquid futures markets to trade and for which CFDs are often available for those retail traders with less risk capital. Specifically, these are coffee, cotton and sugar.

Coffee

Trading coffee may sound like something you might do with a friend at Starbucks. Nevertheless, coffee, unbeknownst to most people, has a key place among the agricultural commodities traded globally. In fact, coffee is the seventh largest agricultural commodity by export value traded on world markets in 2007.

Coffee originates from one of several species of evergreen bush from the Coffea genus. Also, coffee falls into the "soft" commodity category, like cocoa, sugar, cotton or any agricultural commodity that is grown.

For most people's morning cup, of which about 500 billion are consumed each year, coffee beans are harvested from the bush they are grown on and roasted. The two principal types of coffee beans that are sold around the world consist of the Coffea Arabica and the Coffea Canephora varieties.

Coffee futures are a popular means of trading coffee, and they allow producers and buyers to hedge price risk. The sheer size and liquidity of the coffee futures market makes trading coffee futures attractive to many speculators. The rest of this section covers various aspects involved in trading coffee and the production of this important agro-commodity.

Coffee Production

World coffee production for 2006 was almost 8 million metric tons, with the top-ten producers being: Brazil, Vietnam, Columbia, Indonesia, Mexico, India, Ethiopia, Guatemala, Honduras and Peru.

Coffee may be the most popular beverage on the planet and has traditionally been grown by small producers. Numbering over 25 million by some estimates, they tend to rely on the crop for a living.

In Brazil, which is responsible for over 33% of annual world coffee production, over five million people are employed in the cultivation and harvesting of the coffee plant which requires regular attention to be optimally productive.

Coffee Prices

A number of factors impact the price of coffee. Nevertheless, weather and supply and demand account for the most direct influence on prices. Prices per pound for coffee were above $1 for most of the 1970's and 1980's.

Nevertheless, the price of coffee started declining because of several fundamental reasons at the beginning of the 1990's after the end of the Cold War. One significant factor was the collapse of the International Coffee Agreement in 1989, which protected producing countries' interests.

In addition, Vietnam entered the international coffee market in 1994 after the United States lifted sanctions on the country. Now the second-largest coffee producer on a global basis, Vietnam provided an enormous new supply of the commodity into the international market.

That combination of events gradually brought the price of coffee down to $0.41 per pound by 2001. This forced many small producers who could no longer make a living from growing coffee in countries like Brazil and Ethiopia to stop producing coffee altogether and to move into slums in large cities. The price of coffee currently ranges between the $1.30 and $1.40 levels.

Trading Coffee

With respect to actually trading coffee, coffee is one of the most active commodities trading at the Intercontinental Exchange or ICE, which was formerly known as the Coffee, Cocoa and Sugar Exchange.

Coffee futures trade primarily on the floor of the ICE, as well as on their electronic trading platform. The ICE contract has traditionally been the most active futures contract for coffee.

Contracts for coffee futures are also traded on the New York Mercantile Exchange or NYMEX and on the CME's Globex electronic trading platform. Both contracts are for 37,500 pounds of Arabica "C" type coffee. Prices are quoted in U.S. Dollars and the minimum fluctuation is $0.0005 a pound or $18.75 per contract.

Trading coffee has inherent risks, so be sure to know what you are doing if you decide to do any trading in the commodities markets.

Cotton

The term cotton generally refers to the world's most widely-used natural fiber for the production of clothing. Cotton is obtained from a tree or shrub primarily grown in tropical and subtropical regions of Africa, India and the Americas.

The fiber producing part of the plant consists of what is known as a boll, which is a white fluffy ball of natural fiber which grows around the seeds of the cotton tree. The fiber obtained from the bolls after removing the seeds is then spun into a yarn or thread from which the soft breathable cotton cloth is then made. This technique has been used for thousands of years.

The rest of this section covers the definition, cultivation and major world cotton producers as well as futures trading and principal futures markets.

Cultivation

Cotton requires conditions generally found in the subtropics of both the Northern and Southern hemispheres with temperate climate conditions and moderate rainfall. While heavy soil is ideal, the soil need not have a high level of nutrients.

Cultivation of cotton in the Northern hemisphere typically starts between the months of February and June, depending on the conditions. While cotton can be grown in dry areas without irrigation, consistent production and yields can only be assured with proper irrigation.

Care must be taken in the cultivation of cotton however, since improper planting and irrigation can lead to the desertification of farmland.

Major World Cotton Producers

The world's largest cotton producers are China, with an annual production of 34 million bales, and India, with an annual production of 24 million bales. A bale of cotton typically weighs 480 pounds.

After China and India, the world's largest cotton producers are:

- The United States – 12.5 million bales

- Pakistan – 9.8 million bales
- Brazil – 5.5 million bales
- Uzbekistan – 4.4 million bales
- Australia – 1.8 million bales
- Turkey – 1.7 million bales
- Turkmenistan – 1.1 million bales and
- Syria – 1 million bales

Cotton has enormous importance as an agricultural commodity because many developing nations cultivate and produce the commodity. Nevertheless, because of the low price third-world farmers receive for their product, and their inability to compete with developed nations, many small producers have cut down on their production.

The more than 25,000 cotton growers in the United States, the world's largest exporter, receive $25 billion a year in government subsidies.

Cotton Trading

Cotton futures trading occur actively on a global basis via a number of principal exchanges and electronic trading platforms. These currently serve as the main futures markets that facilitate trading cotton as a commodity.

The primary resource for cotton futures is the New York Mercantile Exchange or NYMEX and the CME Group's ClearPort and Globex electronic trading platforms. In addition, the Intercontinental Exchange or ICE also offers a cotton futures contract.

Each futures contract for cotton on both the NYMEX and the ICE covers a trading amount of 50,000 pounds of cotton in a form that is approved by that exchange.

Furthermore, all cotton futures prices traded on the NYMEX and on the ICE will be quoted in U.S. Dollars. Also, the minimum price fluctuation for such cotton futures is $0.0001 per pound. This works out to $5.00 per futures contract.

Sugar

When it comes to trading sugar as a commodity, sugar refers to the common name of a carbohydrate more formally referred to as sucrose. Common sources of sugar include the sugar cane plant and the sugar beet plant.

Sugar generally appears in the form of a white or brown crystalline powder. Also, since sugar is sweet to the taste, many products contain sugar as a natural sweetener. One of sugar's more common uses includes sweetening hot beverages like coffee, tea and cocoa.

Furthermore, sugar is used to sweeten many commercially-produced carbonated soft-drinks, breakfast cereals and dessert foods. Sugar also has an application as an addition to some medicines that otherwise would be unpalatable without the sweetness sugar provides.

This rest of this section covers trading sugar as a commodity including what it is, where its futures trade and on what contract terms.

Sugar Production

Sugar cane is grown all over the world and produces six times more sugar than sugar beets which makes up the second largest source of sugar. Sugar cane is the source for an estimated total world production of 1,600 million metric tons of sugar from 110 countries and accounts for the majority of sugar produced. The world's largest producer of sugar cane is Brazil, followed by India.

Sugar cane production in Brazil is primarily used for the production of ethanol which is a major fuel source in that country. Sugar is 30% more efficient than grains for the production of ethanol.

Other large producers of sugar cane include: Cuba, Peru, Columbia, Bolivia, Australia, Ecuador and El Salvador.

Sugar Cane Processing

Processing sugar cane typically requires two stages. In the first, milling is performed to extract the raw sugar from the sugar cane. Then, the sugar is refined to obtain what is known as refined white sugar which consists of 99% pure sucrose.

Sugar cane is also processed for the production of ethanol which is becoming the main product obtained from the sugar cane plant, even surpassing its use as a sweetener. One hectare of sugar cane produces almost 1,000 gallons of ethanol per year.

Sugar Futures

Trading sugar futures occurs actively on a global basis via a number of principal exchanges and electronic trading platforms. These currently serve as the main futures markets that facilitate trading sugar as a commodity.

The primary resource for trading sugar futures is via the New York Mercantile Exchange or NYMEX and the Chicago Mercantile Exchange or CME Group's ClearPort and Globex electronic trading platforms. The popular food sweetener is actively-traded on that exchange using the symbol YO.

Each futures contract used for trading sugar on the NYMEX covers a trading amount of 112,000 pounds of sugar in a form that is approved by that exchange.

Furthermore, all sugar futures prices traded on the NYMEX will be quoted in U.S. Dollars. Also, the minimum price fluctuation for such copper futures is $0.0001 per pound. This works out to $11.20 per futures contract.

CHAPTER 5: COMMODITY TRADING STRATEGIES

When it comes to being successful as a commodity trader, having the presence of mind to develop a strategy, the mental agility to act quickly in the face of opportunity and the discipline to stick to your plan is priceless.

Research even indicates that the strategic trading mindset is the optimal way to approach trading in virtually any commodity or financial market. The following sections will cover some of the most popular commodity trading strategies so that you can get a sense for which general style might suit you best.

If you feel especially creative, then you can always develop your own strategy, but it will probably still help you to know which ones many traders have previously used successfully.

Day Trading the Commodity Market

This section covers the very popular commodity trading strategy of day trading, including what day trading in the commodity market entails and what strategies are commonly used by day traders.

Day trading will generally suit well those traders who do not like to hold positions overnight. In fact, "short-term is noon" could aptly describe a day trader's frame of mind. Basically, being a day trader, whether in the commodity market or any other market, means that a trader does not take positions home with them.

When Day Traders Trade

As the name implies, a "day trader" in the commodity market really only trades during a specific time frame, which usually encompasses the normal business hours of the main commodity markets in their country. Instead of looking at the big picture, the day trader focuses in on what takes place in the market on the day they trade, not tomorrow and not in a month, but just for that day.

Although commodity CFDs tend to trade around the clock during weekdays at online brokers, each regional commodity futures market has trading hours that you will need to familiarize yourself with by visiting the relevant exchange's website.

Furthermore, certain times of the trading day may seem more advantageous for day traders than others, depending on the commodity involved and the strategy they employ. For example, some commodities often see several hours of higher volatility during the hours that London's business hours overlap with those of New York.

How Day Traders Trade

Typically, a day trader aims to take advantage of one or more intra-day swings in the market, usually getting in and out quickly. Depending on the trading system they use, the day trader will often try to capture one or more intraday swings.

Since day traders look to capitalize on small price moves, the day trader needs volatility in the market to make their trading activities worthwhile. Fortunately, the commodity market lends itself superbly to the needs of day traders and provides ample volatility for day traders to profit from in many major commodity, as well as in the more illiquid secondary commodity markets.

Furthermore, day traders generally rely on technical analysis to determine optimum entry and exit points on price charts. The most commonly-used charts for a commodity day trader are the five-minute, fifteen-minute and one-hour price charts. Of course, many day traders use a variety of other indicators depending on each individual trader's strategy and trading plan.

The way that a day trader will decide on taking a trade usually involves a particular technical indicator or market signal that, once reached, will prompt the trader to take action. As in most effective trading plans, the day trader will optimally initiate a commodity position with clear profit objectives and risk tolerance levels.

To implement this strategy, the trader will generally enter both a stop-loss order to limit their risk, as well as an order to liquidate at a profit once the market attains their objective. Naturally, they will need to cancel the other order once either level is reached, and can sometimes do this automatically with an OCO or one-cancels-the-other order type.

Who Day Trades?

Day trading will not be especially popular with the faint of heart, since the intra-day commodity market price swings can be stressful to some people. Nevertheless, they usually sleep well at night because they have closed out all of their trading positions by then.

Now that small accounts can be readily opened with online brokers that made commodity CFD trading using margin accounts, more and more retail commodity traders find day trading to be a profitable pursuit.

Range Versus Trend Trading Strategies

The debate over range versus trend trading strategies has adherents on both sides in the commodity market, and both strategies have been proven to work extremely well for some people. Since markets sometimes range and sometimes trend, using a combination of the two strategies that are each applied when appropriate can also be quite profitable.

The old market saying: "The trend is your friend," describes the general mindset for trend trading, while range trading can be more suitable for shorter-term traders who like to "buy low and sell high."

This rest of this section contains an explanation of range versus trend trading strategies and how commodity traders can use either or both trading styles successfully.

Trend Traders

Trend traders typically have a trading style where they first identify a particular trend in a commodity's price after a reversal. They then look to subsequently liquidate the position either before the end of the move or just after it ends and reverses slightly.

Accordingly, the trend trader will wait for the next price reversal and will follow the commodity's price movements closely using different technical indicators to alert them of a pending reversal in price direction.

Once identified, the trend generally needs to be confirmed before taking a position. Upon confirmation, a short or long position is established in the direction of the trend along with orders to liquidate the position at pre-determined profit and risk levels.

Often, trend traders will manage their risk by cutting losses and reducing the size of their trades during periods of high volatility in the market. While trend trading is a popular commodity trading strategy, and many people use it successfully, it is not for everyone especially since it usually involves holding positions overnight and even over the weekends when commodity markets do not trade and so pricing gaps can be seen from one week's close to the next week's open.

Furthermore, in the commodity markets, money deposited in brokerage margin accounts can often be leveraged at a substantial ratio depending on the futures exchange or online broker. A leverage ratio of 20 to 1 means that with $100 you can control $2,000 worth of a commodity.

Using this sort of increased leverage, trend traders can make a good deal of money quickly if they catch the right timing on a substantial market trend. Nevertheless, trends can fail, and trading on the wrong side of what looked like a trend can be a costly venture when you are employing leverage that acts like a classic two-edged sword.

Range Traders

In contrast, range traders typically look for non-directional markets that are forming consolidation patterns. As the name implies, their trading style involves trading within a particular price range.

Generally, they will add to long positions at the lower end of the range and increase short positions at the higher end of the range. They will then take profits as the market approaches the opposite side of the range.

A range trader's view on the market is that regardless of where the price is headed, it is bound to return and trade at the same price eventually. Typically, a range trader will prefer to start with an initial trade and then might add to that position if they see a better price using a "doubling up" strategy.

For example, a range trader might start by shorting the WTI Crude Oil near futures contract around where they think is the top of the range is at $60 per barrel and then continue shorting it at intervals of $5, until the price reaches a point near the bottom of the range the perceive in the $45 region. When the futures price subsequently moves down to the $45 region, the range trader will cover their entire short position for a profit.

Trading in this fashion could be extremely capital-intensive, however, and would require deep pockets in order to trade comfortably. A solution to this dilemma is that many brokers offer clients the ability to trade in fractions of a full futures contract amount instead of the customary whole numbers. This is especially useful for smaller retail traders when a commodity has a very high entry price per contract.

Trading in fractions of a futures contract makes each tick in the futures price worth proportionally less and can substantially relieve the pressure of laying out large amounts of money in margin calls to maintain an underwater position.

Basically, by correctly sizing their trading units based on their risk tolerance and account size, a trader can range trade with a smaller amount of money and a lower level of risk that can notably increase their personal comfort level when trading.

The Importance of Discipline and Your Trading Plan

While both range and trend trading strategies differ considerably in style, the commodity market can accommodate both systems profitably depending on the particulars and parameters of the trading system implemented.

Furthermore, trading style tends to takes second seat in terms of importance when compared to having discipline, good money and risk management, and a sound trading plan. Either strategy can work for a disciplined trader with a well-defined and tested trading system. The key seems to be sticking to a trading plan that works, especially when it comes to adhering strictly to any planned stop-losses.

Basically, irrespective of whether you use range versus trend trading strategies, having success when trading depends on your skill in knowing how to plan your trade and your discipline when you trade your plan.

Commodity Swing Trading

Commodity swing trading has proven itself popular as a trading strategy among many commodity traders over the years. The commodity market lends itself particularly well to short-term strategies, and so swing trading can suit traders looking to capitalize on moves in that market that last more than one day.

A swing trader typically looks for price moves of shorter duration, and they will tend to hold a position for one to five days, although in some cases they might stay in a trade for several weeks. This contrasts with a day trader who generally will not hold positions overnight. Swing traders often use a number of different market signals and technical indicators to evaluate the optimum entry and exit points in the market.

This rest of this section will outline some of the more popular commodity swing trading strategies and compare swing trading to other commodity trading strategies.

Swing Trading Strategies

The way that most swing traders evaluate the market depends on levels of support and resistance commonly found within a major trend. Such traders generally wait for a commodity's price to hit resistance or support levels within the major trend.

They might then initiate a new position or add to an existing one once confirmation of the price direction has been made. After such confirmation, the trader will attempt to initiate the position supported by the momentum of the market's resumed direction.

Another swing trading strategy might involve trading against the major trend in the short-term when it looks to be weakening. Such a trader will watch the commodity price move into either a support or a resistance zone in one direction, and they then will take a position that will profit from the commodity price's correction of its initial move. Stops will usually be placed beyond the identified support or resistance zone.

Traders often find swing trading systems relatively easy to develop. A technical analysis plan based on levels of support and resistance, perhaps combined with two other indicators used to confirm the short-term trend, are often all a trader needs.

Kept simple, swing trading can be relatively easier to manage than day trading, but it often requires positions to be held overnight and the trader needs to maintain a disciplined approach to keep losses from getting out of hand.

Swing Trading versus Trend Trading

Swing traders have a somewhat different outlook from trend traders because they will often look to capitalize on price moves contrary to the major trend. On the other hand, trend traders generally look to identify a trend and establish positions on that side of the market to profit from it. Also, trend traders typically hold their positions for a considerably longer period of time.

A trend trader will simply identify the major trend and look for opportunities to initiate a position in that direction, often on a pullback or price correction. A swing trader, on the other hand, will generally identify a trend and watch as levels of support and resistance become clearly defined.

After the swing trader has established levels of support and resistance, a confirmation by another set of indicators is often required before they initiate a trading position. Typically, the indicators might be exponential moving averages or EMA's and/or a certain reading criteria for the Relative Strength Index or RSI that helps traders identify overbought and oversold market conditions. Once the direction has been confirmed by their chosen indicators, the trader will then initiate a position.

As in all good trading plans, swing traders will place stop-loss orders to control risk in the event they turn out to be wrong on the market. They may also place an order to liquidate the position in order to take profits at one or more appropriate levels.

The Grey Area

Swing trading occupies a grey area between day trading and trend trading with respect to trading frequency since traders employing it tend to trade less often than day traders and more often than trend traders. Furthermore, the trading strategy could make a good fit for newer traders and seasoned traders alike as long as they can stomach taking positions overnight.

Although the profits earned with swing trading may not be as large as with trend trading, the strategy generally does not require the amount of activity that day trading requires so commodity trading commissions may be saved that can be a particular benefit to futures traders who tend to pay higher transaction fees than online CFD traders.

Overall, swing trading definitely merits further study and consideration for those willing to take on the risk of holding trading positions overnight.

Scalping and Market-Making Commodities

Many professional commodity traders operate in the commodity markets using strategies known as scalping and market-making. While market making is typically unavailable to the retail trader, some exceptionally quick-witted commodity traders do manage to find success using the scalping strategy.

Still, scalping and market-making in the commodity markets can both be risky trading strategies without the proper amount of discipline. Although both types of commodity traders mainly look to capture the bid/offer spread, the primary difference between them lies in the size of their transactions and whose account they trade for.

The Dealing Spread

In the commodity market, as in just about any other market, bid and offer prices are constantly quoted in the major commodities to accommodate both buyers and sellers. The difference between these prices represents the bid/offer spread, the dealing spread, or just the spread.

In commodity market jargon, "making" or "capturing" the spread means buying the commodity at the bid side price and selling the same commodity at the offer side price, regardless of in which order the transactions get done.

Market-Makers

A professional commodity market-maker, who can either be situated on a futures exchange floor or upstairs in the dealing room of a major financial institution or trading house, is employed by to make prices in commodities. They will usually provide both sides of the rate, or "make a market" to those wishing to deal the commodity contracts they specialize in making markets in.

Over the counter commodity market-makers may quote prices to their professional counterparties, to their customer dealing desk or via electronic broking systems. Irrespective of where the trade will take place, a market-maker's primary interest lies in trading on either side of the price because they look to capture the difference between the bid and offer, i.e. the spread, by buying on the bid side and selling on the offer. They especially like to see high volumes of business with trades made on both sides of the market to make their endeavors more worthwhile.

The width of a market maker's dealing spread will tend to be fairly consistent, except perhaps in especially volatile or "fast" markets. Also, their bid and offer price levels will generally favor one side or the other depending on whether they are more interested in buying or selling based on their current net position or on what they think the client is planning on doing.

For example, if they are already long or they think the client is a seller, then they will tend to show a lower offer and bid. Conversely, if they are already short or think the client is a buyer, they will tend to show a higher offer and bid.

While scalpers generally work for themselves, a market-maker can work for themselves, on a futures exchange, or for a bank or another large financial institution which guarantees the market-maker's trades. In the over-the-counter commodity market, a market-maker can handle multiple commodities. Similarly, market makers operating in futures exchange trading pits can quote prices on multiple commodities, but in practice, they will usually only quote prices on those commodities traded in a single pit.

Making markets in commodities seems relatively easy in comparison to scalping. A market-maker simply quotes both sides of the commodity's price, skewing the market they quote based on their outstanding position or their sense of what the client wants to do, and either they or a clerk keeps a running book of their trades. They also aim to lay off any excessive risk with other counterparties, much like a bookie.

While some market-makers operate as independent traders working for their own account, most commodity market-makers work as salaried employees in futures markets or at large financial institutions. This tends to takes some of the pressure out of this highly active form of commodity trading.

Scalper Trading Methods

Scalpers usually look to capture the spread like market-makers, although scalpers usually are also day traders who trade for their own account. As a result, they trade in much smaller amounts than the large sizes professional market makers typically deal in. Despite their smaller transaction size, scalpers trade the bid/offer spread in much the same way as market makers, usually looking for a quick turnaround on a position.

In essence, scalpers look to get in and out of a trade as fast as possible with a profit. Many scalpers rely extensively on technical analysis to pick optimum times to scalp the market. Generally, the scalper will use one minute, five minute and fifteen minute charts to base their trades on.

In addition to using very short-term price charts, many commodity scalpers use WMAs or weighted moving averages. Such scalpers might look for resistance in an upwards trend or support in a downwards trend that shows up as a double top or double bottom in the weighted moving average. Once this signal manifests, a scalper can then begin initiating positions since the price will tend to oscillate back and forth between the moving averages.

Many commodity market scalpers also use other technical indicators, such as Exponential Moving Averages and Bollinger bands to provide trading signals. Another popular technique used by scalpers involves trading at the opening or closing of major futures markets, such as at the New York Metals Exchange or NYMEX open or at the London Metals Exchange or LME close.

Regardless of what techniques a scalper uses, they usually need to be completely absorbed in watching the market and ready to pull the trigger on any given trade. While scalping may sound easy, few trading strategies are more challenging and require as much concentration, discipline and intense trading activity as scalping.

Commodity Spread Trading

Commodities spread trading can be defined as trading the price differential between two or more commodities futures contracts. Spread trading requires somewhat greater sophistication than normal futures trading, largely because knowledge of each commodity is imperative, if the spread trader expects to be profitable.

Spreads in commodities futures often involve different products of the same basic commodity. For example, some professional traders speculate on spreads such as crude oil against gasoline, which is commonly known as the "Crack Spread", while other spread traders might prefer those on agricultural products like the soybean complex.

The rest of this section discusses commodity spread pricing and describes what is involved in commodity spread trading as a trading strategy.

Why Commodities of Different Months Trade at Different Prices

Commodities generally have carrying costs, in other words, the price for a near-term commodities contract will generally cost less than one that is further out in time because of the costs involved in storing the commodity over time.

For example, a near term futures contract on gold will most likely be less expensive than a contract that is for delivery at a later time. A standard gold contract is usually for 100 ounces of almost-pure gold, and a storage premium will typically be paid for the gold futures contract that has a delivery date six months from the time the contract is purchased. This reflects the carrying and storage costs for the 100 ounces of gold over that period.

Furthermore, if interest rates rise, the carrying cost on the far-term contract will reflect the rise the spread between the near and far-term contracts widening. This example illustrates how a futures contract spread can widen because of an interest rate change that affects the cost of carrying a position.

Other Factors That Influence Commodities Spreads

Each commodity has its own reasons to merit a spread. In agricultural commodities, spreads can widen or narrow depending on inclement weather, as well as on other factors that might affect supply and demand for the commodity.

Also, seasonal factors play a major role in how agricultural commodities contracts can be spread profitably. Corn contracts, for example, typically rise when approaching the December delivery date, while the July contracts usually fall as they approach delivery.

The December contract rises because of an increase in demand for corn during the winter months, while the July contract falls, because of a lower demand for corn during the summer months.

The Soybean Complex

The pricing of some spreads in the commodities market reflect differences in supply and demand of products derived from a basic commodity. Soybeans provide one such example, and soybean contracts can be spread against products that use soybeans for their production such as soybean meal and soybean oil.

Commonly known as the "Crush Spread", this spread involves a trading speculating that the price of soybean oil and meal will change relative to that of the basic soybean product. They would enter this spread by buying or selling the soybean contracts and then simultaneously selling or buying soybean oil and soybean meal contracts against the soybean contracts.

The ratio classically used in this crush spread derives from the fact that one bushel of crushed soybeans will generally produce 11 pounds of soybean oil and 44 pounds of soybean meal. In addition to being traded by speculators, this spread can be used by soybean processors to hedge their production of oil and meal.

Commodity spread trading will generally be performed by more experienced traders since it requires a deeper understanding of the market to be profitable. Nevertheless, margins for spreads are typically lower than for outright futures contract trades, as are the resulting risks and returns.

Using Automated Commodity Trading Software

A relatively recent development in trading the commodity markets involves the use of new technologies like automated commodity trading software. Such programs are especially well suited to trading Contracts for Difference or CFDs on commodities in margin trading accounts available from online brokers via the Internet.

This means just about anyone with even a small amount of money to put at risk can now begin trading in the commodity markets just like the professionals whose expertise is programmed into these often fully-automated algorithmic trading software programs or "trading robots", as they are sometimes called.

Due to its ease of use, automated trading software has become increasingly popular in recent years, and the advantages it offers for both experienced and inexperienced commodity traders are considerable.

Electronic and Automated Trading

Electronic trading has been around for quite some time now and has its origins in the equities market where open outcry-style stock exchanges have gradually given way to automated electronic trading systems that started to become a force to reckon with in the 1980's. This technology was soon applied by enterprising traders to the commodity futures and forex markets once electronic trading became readily available in those markets.

Furthermore, the advent of online trading via the Internet in the past twenty years has brought electronic commodity trading to the masses. In the past few years, automated commodity trading software has become increasingly popular, and for good reason. The main advantage that automated commodity trading programs provide is that the so-called "trading robot" software truly makes trading effortless.

You do not have to watch any screens, have a background in commodity trading, do any exhaustive fundamental research on economics or the weather, or review technical indicators to initiate a trade using a trading robot. The automatic trading software simply comes pre-programmed by experts to analyse the commodity market using objective and effective technical analysis techniques and optimized parameters.

The commodity trading robot will determine entry and exit points, size its positions appropriately, initiate a position automatically, and then place liquidation orders. All of this is done completely automatically, without you having to lift even a finger!

The only thing you have to do is keep your trading account funded if the live trading results do not show the impressive profits found on the robot vendor's sales page, as often seems to be the case. As with many other money-making opportunities that seem too good to be true, trading robots like these often show inconsistent results.

The MetaTrader 4 Trading Platform

With respect to online trading platforms that support automated trading, one especially popular option is known as MetaTrader 4. Also called MT4 for short, this platform is even offered for online download at no charge by its developers MetaQuotes.

MT4 provides real time market pricing, historical data for analysis, and an easy electronic trade execution facility for some of the most popular trading robots available to online traders.

Not only can you purchase an off-the-shelf robot to trade automatically for you using MT4, but you can even use MT4's proprietary MQL 4 programming language to develop your own Expert Advisor or EA to trade a custom trade plan for you.

Getting Your Trading Robot Started

These days, most automated trading software works as an Expert Advisor within an online trading platform like MetaTrader 4 that then interfaces with an online commodity CFD broker that holds your margin account.

To get started trading automatically, you will first need just a few minutes to purchase, download and install the trading robot software of your choice in the directory of a compatible online trading platform on your computer.

The next important step will be to open and fund a trading account with an online CFD broker that will let you trade the commodities you are most interested in. Once the funds hit your trading account, you can start your robot running.

Once activated, the trading robot then advises your trading platform when to initiate a trade based on the pre-programmed trading parameters in the software and the market price action it observes. The robot also places liquidating orders to close any initiated positions out.

At this point, you can just sit back and watch the trading robot's performance as it trades tirelessly for you day and night as long as the commodity CFD market is open and your computer remains online!

Recommendations and Reservations about Using Trading Robots

At present, a considerable number of automated trading software packages can be found for sale online. Nevertheless, many of the available packages seem to optimize their parameters using cherry-picked historical data and then make amazing profitability claims, while at the same time providing disclaimers that future profitability may not be as fabulous.

Accordingly, it can really pay to do some research of your own and test any product you purchase thoroughly if you are serious about using automated trading software to trade commodity CFDs. Also, automated trading robots generally come with programmable variables, and some people have claimed greater success with their robots in terms of profitability by adjusting these parameters.

Another advantage to automated trading software is that virtually all products made for this purpose are based on indicators used in the technical analysis of market price movements. Therefore, a thorough study of the software's trading decisions can give a neophyte a deeper understanding of technical analysis and trading strategies. This is a unique form of a market education that they would not have been able to obtain so easily a few short years ago, other than by watching an expert trader perhaps.

In addition, you can get a free trial for many of these software packages and some of them come with a two-month money back guarantee, so you can use it to demo trade and evaluate the software yourself before you lay out any of your hard-earned cash to set it running on a funded account.

It is strongly recommended that you do a minimal amount of research on both commodity trading and trading software before setting up your margin trading account with an online broker and taking the plunge by letting a robot trade for you without supervision. As world-famous investor Warren Buffet once said, "Risk comes from not knowing what you're doing."

CHAPTER 6: COMMODITY PRICE ANALYSIS

In order to differentiate pure gambling or speculation from strategic trading, a key element involves analyzing the commodity market to determine its most likely future direction. Two primary types of price analysis predominate among traders in today's commodity market, and they are typically known as technical and fundamental analysis.

Technical analysis focuses almost exclusively on market observables like the price and trading volume, while fundamental analysis looks at the relative supply and demand status of the commodity being traded, including the fundamental of any industries and/or manufactured products that the commodity is used in.

Fundamental analysis for commodities can also involve performing a detailed market overview, including production sources, industrial uses, legal, regulatory and weather environments, the stability of established price fixing programs like cartels, and consumer confidence in and demand for the commodity or its downstream products.

Some fundamental commodity analysts will review the prospects for one commodity relative to another to assess whether or not the commodity seems cheap or expensive. In addition to being used to establish outright positions, this type of analysis can be used to establish spread positions where the expensive commodity is sold while the cheaper commodity is purchased.

The following sections will introduce each form of analysis, although a very detailed treatment of these important topics lies beyond the scope of this book and is definitely a worthwhile topic for further reading.

Introduction to Commodity Technical Analysis

In any introduction to technical analysis, perhaps the first thing a commodity trader needs to understand is that fundamental information like supply and demand data, including production and industrial use statistics, generally become rapidly priced or "discounted" into the commodity price once they are commonly available to market-makers. The saying that technical traders often use to encapsulate this concept is: "Price discounts all."

The art and science of technical analysis assumes the truth of this idea, in addition to making the observation that human behavior in crowds tends to repeat itself. Such behavior shows up visually in the price action of a commodity observed over time as market psychology fluctuates between periods of optimism or bullishness on the commodity and times of pessimism or bearishness.

As a result of the foregoing assumptions, the trader basing their decisions on technical analysis can ignore all of the otherwise distracting market information. Instead, they can focus their attention on using the commodity price and its past behavior to forecast its future direction, often with impressively accurate results.

Some of the more popular technical analysis techniques and a brief description follow:

- **Chart Patterns**

    Chart patterns seem to arise because the human behavior that drives markets tends to repeat itself. In general, chart patterns tend to fall into the basic categories of continuation, reversal or consolidation patterns, depending on how the subsequent price action usually proceeds once the pattern completes itself.

    A major advantage of technical analysis arises from the fact that many of these chart patterns provide specific "measuring objectives" in terms of price and even sometimes with respect to time when a particular trigger level is broken. As a result, once they identify a reliable chart pattern, the technical commodity trader can operate in the market with a considerably greater degree of objectivity.

- **Trends and Channels**

Trends form an especially important class of continuation chart pattern. Technical analysts generally identify an uptrend by a series of higher highs and higher lows in the price, and a down trend by a set of lower lows and highs. Furthermore, sets of parallel lines can sometimes be drawn through the identifying high and low reversal points to define a channel that the price is moving within.

Once the price breaks an established channel in a direction contrary to the initial trend, that event signals the end of the trend. It also sets up a price objective equal to the width of the channel projected from the point of penetration.

- **Support and Resistance**

    By looking at a chart of price movements over time, a technical analyst can identify places where buying interest overcame selling interest to prompt a bullish reversal in price action, or where selling interest surpassed buying interest to prompt a bearish reversal.

    These levels would be known as support and resistance levels respectively, because buying interest supports the price, while selling interest generally provides resistance to a move higher.

- **Technical Indicators**

    Another major area of technical analysis involves using one or more of the wide variety of technical indicators available to analyze price or volume data numerically. Such indicators usually provide clear trading signals that traders often incorporate into their trading plans.

    An example of one of the more popular indicators is the Relative Strength Index or RSI. The RSI gives insight into whether the market is oversold or overbought and hence due for a consolidation or reversal.

    Another classic technical indicator is the Moving Average that smoothes out the price action and provides useful information about the prevailing trend and possible reversals.

Using Technical Analysis to Trade Commodities

When it comes to using technical analysis to trade commodities, a wide variety of choices are readily available that could suit either the novice or more advanced trader.

Some of the more popular of these technical trading choices appear below in approximate order of the complexity involved in implementing them.

Read a Technical Newsletter

Perhaps the easiest way that a novice trader could start using technical analysis to trade commodities would be to start reading a technical analysis newsletter written by expert technical analysts.

This way, they would receive the ongoing directional advice of professionals working in the field. Then, as they read the newsletter over time, they can gradually attempt to replicate the analytical results that the technical pros provided.

Subscribe to a Trade Signal Generating Service

A relatively modern development in commodity trading involves using technical trading signal services. These companies generally provide commodity market trade signals that are automatically generated based on trade plans developed by experts. Such signal services are offered to the public as commercial products for either a one-time fee or on an ongoing payment basis.

You can simply subscribe to one of these services by paying their fees, and they will provide you with technical trading signals. Signal service subscribers can sometimes set up funded margin accounts to automatically trade on such signals given risk parameters they prefer, or they can more commonly manually decide whether or not to place a trade based on the signals they receive and how much to place at risk on each trade.

Educate Yourself about Technical Analysis Methods

Many good books have been written about technical analysis, including John Murphy's classic book entitled "Technical Analysis of the Financial Markets" that many professional traders consider the best reference on the subject. That reference and others are mentioned in the Recommended Further Reading portion of this book contained in Chapter 11.

Also, the Internet hosts plenty of online educational material on a variety of websites about using technical analysis to trade commodities and other financial markets. Another idea is to read through the help file on your charting software for each technical indicator or charting tool you think you might be interested in using.

Finally, if you happen to have personal access to an experienced technical analyst, then they can probably provide you with some helpful analytical tips to get you started on the right foot when it comes to applying technical analysis to your trading activities.

Obtain a Charting Service

For those who want to start doing their own technical analysis, perhaps the most important thing do-it-yourself technical traders need is charting software. Your essential charting program should not only provide up-to-date prices for commodities you will need to analyze, but it should also feature the ability to:

- View high and low points on the chart.
- Plot bar and candlestick chart types.
- Chart different periods, including hourly, daily and weekly.
- Draw trend lines, channels and horizontal lines.
- Allow chart annotations.
- Superimpose indicators you want to use and read levels.
- Save charts and templates for future reference.

Fortunately, most online trading platforms will include charting and technical indicators as part of its core functionality, along with real time prices and a database of historical prices for the most popular commodities. For example, MetaTrader includes excellent charting features and costs nothing to download and use if you wish to use it for online CFD trading via a broker that supports it.

Develop a Successful Technical Trade Plan

By learning from the experience of others, and perhaps also by experimenting with different technical indicators and analysis methods, persistent traders using technical analysis to trade commodities usually eventually come up with a winning trade plan.

Naturally, your trade plan does not have to win on every trade it suggests, provided of course that it generates bigger winning trades than losing trades over the long term. Back-testing your plan over historical price data can help you assess its past success, although this does not guarantee its future success, of course.

Automate Your Technical Trade Plan

As traders advance in applying their technical analysis skills and develop a successful and objective technical trading plan when using technical analysis to trade, many increasingly wish to program a computer to do all of the trading for them so that they can sit back and relax. What was once only a trader's dream has now become possible in reality!

Some novice traders might prefer to use commercial trading robot software for this purpose, but more advanced traders can now either program or have programmed their own personalized automated trading software that can execute commodity deals automatically through many online CFD brokers using trading platforms like MetaTrader.

Trading Using Technical Indicators

Technical indicators rely solely on levels of supply and demand and can give traders experienced in reading them a clear picture of where the market has been. Nevertheless, technical indicators can only give a probable sense of future direction, not a guarantee.

The rest of this section covers the most popular technical indicators for traders and gives an overview on their usefulness.

Popular Technical Indicators

Most market professionals who take strategic positions will use market indicators regularly to gauge the market and also to base their trading decisions upon. Some of the most common technical indicators used in trading and a brief description of their trading signals follow below:

- **Moving Averages** – a Simple Moving Average or SMA takes the price observed over a period of time and calculates an average price. The SMA will generally lag the price over the calculation period, which is why some technicians prefer to use the Exponential Moving Average or EMA instead. The EMA gives more weight to recent prices relative to older prices and so seems more responsive to price action. Moving averages generate buy signals when a short-term average moves above a longer-term one, and sell signals are generated when the longer-term average exceeds the shorter.

- **Relative Strength Index or RSI** – an indicator that will indicate an oversold market under 30 and an overbought market over 70. The RSI can offer a trader a good sense of when a market might be due for a correction or reversal.

- **Directional Movement Indicator or DMI** – this indicator varies on a scale of 0 to 100 and shows a higher reading when a market trends. The indicator has a positive component the +DI that shows the strength of an upwards trend, and a negative component (-DI) that indicates how strong a downward trend is. The indicator generates trade signals when the +DI and –DI cross. When the +DI exceeds the –DI, a bullish trend predominates, and when the –DI is higher than the +DI, a bearish trend prevails.

- **Volume Indicators** – the volume of trading is a market observable that provides extremely important information to technical traders because it gives indications of how strong a rally or how weak a decline has become. Also, increasing volume often confirms a break out of a consolidation chart pattern, so volume indicators will typically be consulted by those trading such chart patterns.

Learn How to Use Technical Indicators

Learning how to begin trading using technical indicators can be one of the best things a trader can do to improve their results, especially if they are relatively new to trading. Basically, developing a strong technical analysis background can provide both invaluable insights and considerably greater objectivity when trading. As a result, technical analysis provides one of the key elements involved in devising profitable trading systems, with another important component being sound money management.

In addition, with the help of recent technological innovations, a trader can now easily isolate technical indicators, overlay them on price charts, and even program new parameters, often using their online trading platform.

Once a trade plan has been developed, some of the more sophisticated trading platforms with algorithmic trading capabilities can even be programmed to automatically enter orders once conditions have been met based on the technical indicators and other trading parameters specified.

Nevertheless, learning how to use technical indicators for trading makes up just one part, albeit an important one, in the development of a successful trader. For most manual traders, you will want to find the indicators that tell you what you want to know about the market and stick to them.

Naturally, you will also want to avoid the pitfall of using too many technical indicators and thereby complicating your trading process unnecessarily if you plan on doing your analysis manually, although numerous indicators can be programmed into an automated trading system or trade signal generation system.

Generating Commodity Trading Signals

Generating trading signals usually involves performing one or more types of technical analysis. Therefore, the first step in learning how to generate signals involves learning about the various technical analysis techniques and how they can be applied to a trading strategy profitably.

Furthermore, a good trading system will not only generate trading signals, but will also give a trader clear indications of where to get in, where to get out profitably and where to admit their trade went wrong so that the position should then be closed out for a loss.

Observing price patterns, technical indicators, and support and resistance levels comprise some of the most common ways to generate commodity trading signals, and each of these techniques enjoy a wide following.

Those new to trading typically need to learn how experts generate trading signals to assist them in trading the commodity market profitably. An explanation and example for each of these useful technical analysis techniques appears below.

Chart Patterns

Price charts have been used by traders to forecast the future direction of financial markets for decades. When these charts became readily available to traders, many of them would look for classic patterns that would reflect the mass psychology behind the supply and demand reflected in the market's prices.

Most of these patterns have points that, when breached, generate a price objective at which to take profits in addition to a stop loss level. These points on the chart allow traders to take on positions objectively with clear levels in mind to take their profits at and manage their risk of loss at.

This type of signal generation usually requires human interpretation to detect the pattern on the chart in the first place, although computers are getting much better when it comes to pattern detection in recent years. Computers can also offer considerable assistance to traders in both charting the prices and also in calculating the likely price objectives.

Technical Indicators

Perhaps the most popular way of generating trading signals involves using technical indicators, and this has already been discussed in previous sections. Various market observables determine the value of these indicators such as price, volume, historical volatility and open interest, when applicable.

Some of the indicators that a trading system might take into account when generating commodity trading signals might include:

- Moving averages – the price average over a set period, for example 5, 10, 30 or even 200 days.

- Relative Strength Index or RSI indicating an overbought market over 70 and oversold market under 30.

- Price action nearing the top or bottom of a Bollinger Band.

The above trading signals comprise some of the more widely-followed and popular indicators. An in-depth study of technical analysis will provide the trader with still other useful indicators that can generate trading signals.

A trading system based on technical indicators also usually applies a set of criteria whereby a buy signal, a sell signal or a do nothing signal would be generated when certain levels are reached and/or conditions observed.

Support and Resistance

"Buy low and sell high" has often jokingly been considered the prime directive when trading, with the amusing factor behind this common statement being that this is by far easier said than done. Nevertheless, by making a detailed visual study of past price reversal points on a chart, a technical analyst can get a good idea of what price levels on the chart people would be willing to buy or sell at.

For example, the so-called "support levels" below the current market price indicate where traders might have placed purchase orders or simply shown prior buying interest, either to establish long position or to take profits and cover short positions. These levels get their name because they support the market and prevent the market from moving lower.

Conversely, the price levels above the prevailing price where sellers emerge to take profits on long positions or go short the market are commonly known as "resistance levels." They get their name since the price has moved up sufficiently to attract sellers that provide resistance to the market moving higher.

A trading plan could be created to generate trading signals based on support and resistance levels. Such a plan might involve buying ahead of key support levels and selling ahead of where the market finds resistance.

Stop-loss orders could be placed comfortably below the support levels and above resistance levels. Conversely, orders to take profits could then be placed below the resistance levels and above support levels.

Useful Chart Patterns

As has already been noted, a number of useful chart patterns can help traders profit from their technical analysis. In general, such chart patterns tend to fall into the basic categories of continuation, consolidation and reversal patterns.

The classification of a chart pattern depends on how the subsequent price action usually proceeds once the pattern completes itself. Triangles present something of an exception because they can break out in either direction, and so can be either continuation or reversal patterns, so their status is typically determined after a breakout is noted.

These categories and some of the useful chart patterns within them are described further in the subsections below.

Continuation and Consolidation Patterns

As the name implies, a continuation pattern is one that signals that the market price will continue again in the same direction once the pattern has completed. These patterns could also be called consolidation patterns since they tend to represent a pause in the general direction of the market as it consolidates after its recent move.

Volume tends to decrease as the market takes a temporary breather, and it then rises again upon a breakout. Examples of common continuation patterns include:

- **Triangles** – These patterns come in symmetrical, ascending and descending types. The market typically trades in a gradually narrower range between converging trend lines before breaking out on increased volume and continuing in that direction. Although certainly a consolidation pattern, as noted earlier, a triangle can be either a continuation or a reversal pattern, depending on which side its breakout occurs on. Triangles generally consist of five increasingly smaller internal movements, and they must break out before reaching their apex. A breakout sets up measuring objective equal to the width between the converging trend lines that define the pattern at the initial high or low.

- **Flags** - Preceded by a sharp move, often called the "flagpole", the market consolidates between parallel trend lines that often slant counter-trend, before resuming sharply in its original direction, and to a similar extent to the original move.

- **Pennants** – Also preceded by a sharp "flagpole" move, in this pattern the market consolidates between converging trend lines, usually resembling a small symmetrical triangle, before resuming sharply in its original direction and to a similar extent to the original move.

- **Wedges** – Consists of two converging trend lines. A falling wedge pattern interrupts an uptrend, and its breakout is bullish, while a rising wedge interrupts a down trend and its breakout is bearish.

- **Rectangles** – A trading range pattern bordered by roughly horizontal lines drawn among the major highs on the top and among the major lows on the bottom. A breakout in either direction sets up a measured move equal to the width of the rectangle.

Reversal Patterns

Signs of a reversal pattern forming provide a good clue that the market may be about to turn and move in the opposite direction. Examples of common reversal patterns include:

- **Head and Shoulders Top or Bottom** – One shoulder forms, then a head forms a major top or bottom, then another shoulder appears at a similar level to the first. The dips or rallies between the head and the shoulders define a neckline. When the neckline breaks, look for a move equal to the distance between the neckline and the head.

- **Double Top or Bottom** – This pattern forms when two tests of a roughly similar level occur, with an intervening dip or rally. The dip or rally defines the neckline and a break of that level sets up a measured move equal to the distance between the neckline and the double peak or trough.

- **Triple Top or Bottom** – Like the double top pattern but with three peaks or troughs instead of two.

- **Triangles** – Please refer to the previous entry under continuation patterns above for triangles which become reversal patterns when their breakout comes in the opposite direction to the preceding trend.

Technical Analysis Software

The term "technical analysis software" used to just refer to programs that charted market price action and allowed traders and technical analysts to draw trend lines and superimpose technical indicators.

Recently, however, the trading world has been transformed by trade signal generator software, computerized chart pattern matching software, and other sophisticated computer-assisted algorithms for analyzing price movements.

This article describes some of the basic types of technical analysis software and what benefits each of them offer to the technical trader.

Charting Technical Analysis Software

Perhaps the most important technical analysis software for the do-it-yourself technical analyst will be charting software. Such a program will need to provide real-time price, as well as historical prices for each of the commodities you want to analyze observed at a variety of time frames.

Such software will probably also include features like the following:

- Plot different chart types including bar and candlestick charts
- View prices on charts and indicators by putting your cursor over them
- Chart different time periods including hourly, daily and weekly price data
- The ability to plot trend lines, flat lines and channels over prices
- Permit the user to notate charts
- Include a variety of popular technical indicators
- Allow for charts and chart templates to be saved for later use.

Fortunately, most online trading platforms include charting software, and some online CFD trading platforms even allow you to execute trades directly from charts, which can be a significant time saving feature.

Pattern-Matching Technical Analysis Software

Analytical chart pattern recognition software programs of this type often use artificial intelligence algorithms to analyze technical analysis charts graphically. For example, this relatively-recent type of technical analysis software might use advanced pattern-matching algorithms to identify traditional and reliable chart patterns on commodity price charts using historical data.

Some of these programs even indicate how certain they are about the pattern, as well as what its trigger points and objectives are. Other programs of this type focus on implementing specific charting techniques like those involved in Elliott Wave Theory analysis, for example.

Although these pattern-matching programs probably cannot yet outperform an experienced human technical analyst, they can usually help a novice identify common chart patterns and compute measuring objective targets, as well as alert an experienced trader to possible trading opportunities that they can then personally analyze in greater detail.

Trade Signal Generating Software

Now available from several commercial vendors, trade signal generating technical analysis software has become increasingly popular of late. Although the software generally falls short of actually executing the deals it recommends for you, it usually provides an audible signal along with a trade recommendation including information like:

- Which asset to trade
- In what direction to take the trade
- Where to liquidate the position at a profit
- Where to close the trade out at a loss if the market takes a turn for the worse.

In practice, trading signal generation software programs typically review one or more of the popular technical analysis indicators for each of the markets that a trader is interested in. The software then provides some sort of audible or visual signal to the trader when a well-defined trading opportunity is present. The software also usually tells traders in what direction to initiate a position and where to place stop loss and take profit orders.

Automated Trading Software

Trading robot software is a completely automated form of algorithmic trading program that was often considered the "holy grail" by traders of the past. Such programs usually base their trading decisions on some form of technical analysis and can also have parameters set by the user.

Nevertheless, most developers would tend to admit that the commercially available trading robot software packages have yet to create unlimited profits for their users without also subjecting them to uncomfortable periods of losses.

A considerable number of software packages are available online with robotic trading abilities that can be set to pick trades automatically. Although automated trading software is admittedly more readily available for the forex market than for commodity trading, online CFD traders can also probably use the same software if they are employing MetaTrader as a trading platform since most trading robots currently operate as an Expert Advisor or EA within MetaTrader.

Nevertheless, many of the more exotic commodity products do not lend themselves to automated trading because of a lack of liquidity and perhaps also because many such assets are strongly-influenced by key fundamental factors like geopolitical, economic, news and supply/demand events that might not be as easy to obtain information about on a timely basis as for a major traded commodity.

Also, many of the automated systems which provide the best results for trading have not yet been released for popular consumption. They are typically used by major investment banks, hedge funds and other commodity trading firms that trade for profit and do not want to lose their edge. Automated trading of CFDs by small retail traders has only recently become readily available, so considerable opportunities for development in that sector exist.

Regardless of whether you seek to trade using a swing, trend or day-trading strategy, a variety of technical analysis software products can provide you with useful trading signals and analytics. While most may not yet be fully-automated for trading, they still can be extremely beneficial in the volatile world of commodity trading and may help you watch markets and identify opportunities that you would otherwise be oblivious to.

Why Technical Analysis Works

Those new to trading may wonder why technical analysis works so well to predict future price levels. They might question why just looking at the basic price data or trading volume levels over time can have any predictive value whatsoever. They also might also not understand how to use the various technical indicators that involve quantitatively assessing some aspect of how prices change, or why such indicators can yield useful trading signals.

This healthy sort of skepticism makes perfect sense to novice traders first exposed to the more advanced topic of technical analysis. Nevertheless, many more experienced traders swear by the effectiveness and efficiency of using technical analysis to predict future prices, as well as its ability to provide objective trade entry and exit points.

As a result, technical analysis has taken a permanent place aside fundamental analysis as an established way of looking at and forecasting future commodity price movements. The rest of this section discusses the theoretical basis for using technical analysis to trade commodities.

An Explanation

Although many people have attempted to explain why technical analysis works, often in quite different ways, perhaps the best explanation arises from the idea that the prices seen in the commodity market represent the equilibrium point at which buying pressure equals selling pressure for the commodity involved. If either buyers or sellers start to predominate, the price will move appropriately, i.e. up or down respectively.

Furthermore, the flow of information into the consciousness of the market's many participants tends to occur efficiently as a result of news services and real-time pricing. As a result, the prices seen in the commodity markets respond rapidly to new relevant events as they occur, and they even take into account or "discount" events that are rumored to be about to occur.

This means that the prices observed soon discount all of the available information pertaining to each commodity, and the market prices do this efficiently and on a continuous basis. This general concept underlies what a technical analyst intends to communicate when they say: "Price discounts all."

Why Read the News??

Most personal traders do not have the time, information systems, background or inclination to be reading detailed commodity reports, scanning news wires for the latest news flashes, or constantly having their finger on the pulse of the market like a professional market-maker might need to. They generally want to have a life instead.

Using technical analysis can provide a workable solution for such armchair traders. All they have to do is make the reasonable assumption that all such available information gets quickly priced into the market by the trading pros whose job it is to do so.

This really takes the pressure off when it comes to watching the news. Basically, if an information release comes out as expected, the observed price will most likely not change much because the information has probably already been discounted by the market.

On the other hand, if the information release notably deviates from what is expected, then the market may initially move in the appropriate direction as market makers short the price to discount the new information.

The main exception to this is when rumors precede the fact, and in that case, the market may retrace much of its initial reaction in a somewhat counter intuitive manner as those who traded on the rumor subsequently take profits when it becomes officially known as fact. As the old market saying goes, "Buy the rumor, sell the fact."

Human Behavior Repeats Itself

Besides the assumption that the prevailing price takes into account all available relevant information, the other fundamental reason why technical analysis works has to do with the repeatability, and hence predictability, of human behavior when people act as a group.

The crowd mentality seen operating in financial marketplaces tends to demonstrate certain patterns of behavior, which in turn show up visually in price movements plotted over time.

Since these observable price patterns tend to repeat themselves time and time again, the results can help forecast the future behavior of market prices. While that may indeed be true, the trick to this form of technical analysis lies in first correctly identifying which pattern the market is trading in and then noting when it breaks out of that pattern.

Using Fundamental Analysis to Trade Commodities

Fundamental analysis of a commodity generally involves going over the commodity's supply and demand profile. Some analysts may also review relevant data for related or competing commodities, as well as information for the economy as a whole, including economic indicators, government fiscal policies, social and political factors, natural disasters, and interest and inflation rates.

Even the weather reports are relevant fundamental information for some commodities, such as those produced by agricultural concerns since adverse weather conditions can affect supply.

Fundamental analysis uses such information as a way of forecasting price trends. While this technique commonly appeals to those traders with an education in economics, business, accounting or corporate finance, just about anyone can learn to determine what fundamental factors move the commodity markets.

This detailed form of analysis allows commodity traders to get a sense of how one commodity is valued relative to another similar commodity in its sector and to the commodity market as a whole. They can then take that into account given the future prospects for supply and demand in order to develop a view on the commodity's future price.

The rest of this section will describe the basics of fundamental analysis and how to use its techniques to trade commodities.

Fundamental Analysis Introduced

In the world of commodities trading, fundamental analysis for commodities involves reviewing the factors directly impacting commodity prices on a regular basis. The fundamentals affecting commodity prices depend on things like:

- The nature of the commodity,
- The supply and demand of the commodity in question,
- Weather impacting major agricultural areas,
- The political stability of the region where the commodity is mined, produced or grown, and
- Other macroeconomic factors.

Commodities make up a large group of different types of resources. Some commodities require mining for example like gold, iron, silver, etc. Others are grown such as grains, beans, fruits and spices, while still others come from drilling like crude oil and natural gas.

Furthermore, some commodities are elaborated or manufactured from other commodities. These might include products like unleaded gasoline, soybean oil, steel and plastics, to name just a few. Other commodities are raised such as cattle and hogs.

Each different type of commodity can be affected by a different set of factors or fundamentals, and fundamental traders typically analyze these different factors to help them determine the most likely overall future direction in commodity prices.

Although a detailed treatment of fundamental analysis is beyond the scope of this introductory book, some of the principal factors in the fundamental analysis for commodities will be covered at a basic level in the following sections.

Supply and Demand

The underlying reason for all commodities price movements involves the ubiquitous forces of supply and demand. This particular factor in the fundamental analysis for commodities has to do with the production and consumption respectively of a given commodity.

Take oil for example. If the world's production of oil begins to lag because of dwindling reserves in Saudi Arabia for example, or if the war in the Middle East expanded, this would invariably increase the price of oil. In turn, this would thereby increase the prices of a myriad of other products elaborated with oil because of rising transportation costs due to higher oil prices.

By the same token, if an electric car was suddenly popularized and a quarter of all cars sold were electric, this would also impact the price of oil. Presumably, gasoline consumption would be drastically cut as a result, and so crude oil prices would plummet.

Weather

In general, all agricultural commodities are subject to weather conditions. If an unseasonable freeze hits a crop, this will invariably impact the commodity price, as will an unseasonable heat wave or a flood.

Basically, such extreme weather conditions will tend to increase prices of agricultural commodities, while ideal conditions and a favorable crop and harvest will adversely impact the price due to raised expectations of an increased supply.

Political Factors

A number of political factors potentially impact commodities prices such as elections, political stability of a commodity-producing country, as well as wars and domestic political problems.

Strikes and labor disputes can also directly affect the levels of supply, especially in a commodity such as copper or coal, while a coup d'état or change in political regime could disrupt entire commodity-producing nations.

Economic Factors

The value of money and interest rates also has considerable influence on commodity prices. If interest rates increase, the storage, maintenance and production costs for many commodities rises, thereby directly affecting prices.

Conversely, with lower interest rates, the cost of production decreases and in effect makes commodities prices lower. Inflationary and deflationary cycles, as well as the economic health of individual commodity producer and consumer nations, often have a strong influence on what commodity prices will be.

How Currencies can Affect Commodity Prices

Since market prices represent the equilibrium balance point between supply and demand in the commodity expressed in a particular national fiat currency, the resulting price also reflects the commodity's value relative to that of the currency in which it is quoted.

Another currency-related factor is that some industrial users of commodities import them from other countries. This means they may have considerable exchange rate risks that can affect their choices of what commodity to use in producing goods for sale.

Accordingly, another fundamental factor is the relative valuation prospects of the national currency that the commodity is traded in. As a result, fundamental data relevant to that quotation currency can also be reviewed by an analyst when attempting to predict directional movements for the commodity's price.

Why Use Fundamental Analysis?

Basically, fundamental analysis for commodities trading can be quite beneficial for novice and seasoned traders alike. It also really helps newer traders get a deeper understanding of the factors that move the markets they are considering trading.

In addition, many traders use fundamental analysis to assess the prospects for long term price movements while using technical analysis to time market entry and exit points.

Used together, fundamental and technical analysis can help a trader get a more complete picture about a commodity's future prospects, and so it is well worth investing time in learning how to analyze fundamental information relevant to commodities if you want to trade them successfully.

Fundamental Data for Commodities

Fundamental analysis of a commodity generally involves going over the commodity's production supply and commercial use demand profile in detail. Production analysis for soft commodities tends to look at the conditions faced by farmers, while for hard commodities analysts tend to look at what miners are experiencing.

Fundamental traders also often pay particular attention to factors that might result in industrial users or consumers preferring one commodity over another in an effort to identify commodity spread trades by finding commodities that are over or under priced relative to others.

The release dates of key information about the economy, inflation and interest rates, and even the weather that might affect a particular commodity are also closely monitored by commodity analysts and traders. Such releases can involve considerable market volatility if the actual release differs significantly from the market's consensus expectation.

Key Economic Data

The release dates of key economic numbers that pertain to the economy as a whole where commodities are traded are widely tabulated in economic calendars. The list below includes most of the key economic data releases that reporting agencies within the various countries provide to the market on a regular basis as indicated.

- **Employment Data** – Released monthly
- **Gross Domestic Product (GDP)** – Released quarterly
- **Trade Balance** – Released monthly
- **Retail Sales** – Released monthly
- **Industrial Production** – Released monthly
- **Consumer Price Index (CPI)** – Released monthly
- **Producer Price Index (PPI)** – Released monthly.

Note that the precise times when such releases occur can result in considerable market volatility if the actual number released differs significantly from what the market is expecting as market-makers scramble to discount the new information into the price.

Other Types of Fundamental Information

In addition to the aforementioned economic data, some of the other important fundamental information commonly used by traders and economists in performing fundamental analysis might include the following:

- Interest and inflation rate levels
- Supply and demand effects relevant to a particular commodity
- Political influences
- Geopolitical events
- Commodity prices
- Survey results
- The Commitment of Traders or COT positioning reports.

Weather and Commodities Prices

As mentioned briefly in previous sections, weather and weather related issues can directly influence prices of a wide variety of commodities. The first and most obvious weather risk involves agriculture. Weather has been a key element in the growing of crops since agriculture began thousands of years ago.

The rest of this section gives an overview of how weather can affect commodities prices.

Weather and Agricultural Commodities

Crops need several basic things to be successful, and one of them involves good weather. Having good weather will increase the yield a farmer will have at harvest and also increases the overall supply of the agro-commodity. This scenario repeated by thousands of farmers results in a bumper crop in that agro-commodity, making the price of the agro-commodity plummet.

On the other hand, an unseasonable rainy season or a prolonged winter storm for example could destroy a large portion of the agro-commodity crop reducing supplies and consequently driving the price higher.

Weather also plays a key role in the transporting of commodities and the ability of producers to get their products to market. An important and often overlooked way that the weather can directly influence commodity prices involves transportation costs, because prices rise when transportation costs rise.

Oil, Transportation and Weather-Related Consumption

Transportation of goods and commodities depends directly on the price of oil to fix shipping costs. While railways still account for a sizeable portion of shipping, trucks and ships which use diesel and gasoline make up a large percentage of the shipping industry. The price of oil also impacts many by-products of the petroleum industry such as plastics and petrochemicals for example.

Inclement winter weather drives demand for heating oil up as well as natural gas, coal and other fuels used for heating homes and buildings. A prolonged cold spell or heavy snowfall directly impacts consumption of many commodities and hence affects the supply, driving prices higher.

Other Weather Considerations

When weather in China destroys the wheat crop due to an early monsoon season, U.S. wheat prices can skyrocket. Furthermore, adverse weather in South America can positively affect the price of coffee, and prolonged droughts can affect the price of most affected agricultural commodities, usually causing prices to rise due to their presumed future scarcity.

When Hurricane Katrina hit the U.S. Gulf Coast, many oil refineries were temporarily knocked out of commission affecting gasoline prices worldwide. The price of gasoline in the United States rose considerably until supplies were later secured from other sources, bringing prices back down.

Weather affects us all directly, and in many cases will affect the food you put on your table, the gas that runs your car and the price you pay for a cup of coffee. Basically, weather can affect entire economies and can hinder or prosper a society like no other single factor.

Many professional commodities traders study weather patterns to get an edge on their trading. Weather has become such a decisive factor in the world commodities market that an industry for trading weather futures has emerged. Commodities traders and other speculators can now trade and hedge the weather risk of their positions with futures contracts on the weather in the commodity producing region.

Macroeconomic and Political Commodity Price Factors

Outside of the effects that weather and natural disasters have on commodities prices, macroeconomics and political reasons for commodities prices tend to be the second main cause for price movements in the commodities markets. History offers many instances of how political and macroeconomic events have directly influenced the prices of commodities.

In fact, just open up a newspaper to see the latest news from the Middle East or Venezuela to get an idea about how the price of a barrel of oil might be changing based on a political event. You can also review current Consumer Price Index readings that gauge inflation to see how they impact the price of gold.

The rest of this section discusses how macroeconomics and political events can influence commodities prices.

Political Events

Since commodities typically consist of food, raw materials or manufactured products, a great deal of human energy must be expended in the production, distribution and storage of commodities. Therefore, if political uncertainty looms in a region that either produces or manufactures a commodity, disruption in its supply may ensue, thereby creating a shortage.

For example, unrest in the Middle East offers the most immediate example of how political events can directly influence commodities prices. During both times that the United States went to war with Iraq, initially in 1990 and again in 2003, the prices of crude oil, gasoline and heating oil all rose. When supply sources were reestablished or new sources found, the commodities prices then declined.

Another way that politics can directly affect commodities prices is during election periods. Consider the example of a commodity-producing country with a large industrial base centered on a particular commodity such as copper. If elections are held in that country, the risk of nationalization of that commodity can affect not only the price of copper, but the share prices of the foreign corporations that previously had an interest in the industry in that country.

Such was the case in Chile in 1970 with the election of Salvador Allende. As a left-wing socialist, Allende nationalized the copper industry and subsequently died in a coup d'état in 1973. Other notable nationalizations have involved the oil reserves in Mexico in the 1930s and also those in Venezuela in the 1970s.

Macroeconomic Reasons for Commodity Price Shifts

Commodity prices have fallen under significant pressure since the 1980s when many third-world producers of a large number of different commodities, as well as the nations of Eastern Europe and the Russian Republic, began exporting their goods.

While a healthy world demand was ready to absorb the surplus, commodity prices declined nevertheless. In general, they have shown weakness ever since, with some notable exceptions like gold and oil.

Macroeconomic news affects commodities prices in a variety of ways. Some elements affect all commodities uniformly such as interest rates, while other factors that can directly influence commodity prices include:

- Where the commodities-producing country is in its business cycle
- A country's money supply
- Whether the overall price situation is inflationary or deflationary
- Gross Domestic and National Product
- Currency exchange rates
- The general level of economic activity.

Macroeconomics and politics can therefore be acknowledged as principal factors in the market's pricing of commodities since they relate directly to the global market forces of supply and demand. As a result, most professional commodity traders keep a watchful eye on political events and economic numbers to obtain an edge in their trading.

Using Fundamentals in Practice

When performing a fundamental analysis on a particular commodity, traders will look at as many fundamental factors as possible for producers and users operating within the relevant economy or economies if cross-border trade is common for that particular commodity. Analysts will take all this data into account, as well as the strength of the currency the commodity is denominated in, when making their price recommendations and trading decisions.

Fundamental traders do this in order to obtain a broad sense of what a particular commodity market's internal, economic and political operating climate is, as well as to determine what growth opportunities exist with respect to demand for the commodity and whether it is suitably valued relative to its competitors.

Basically, if the fundamental data looks better for the commodity relative to others it competes with, then that would tend to imply a rising forecast for its price relative to its competitors. On the other hand, if the commodity's data comes across as weaker relative to others it competes with, then a falling forecast would tend to ensue for its market price relative to its competition.

The commodity's price might still rise in a rising market, especially if inflation is high and the currency in which it is denominated is weak, but probably not as much as other commodities that offer better value. A neutral forecast would tend to result when prospects are roughly the same on balance for commodity relative to others it competes with given their pricing, as long as the underlying market is stable.

Once having made such a forecast, the fundamental commodity trader would then look for opportunities to position themselves in the market to take advantage of the forecast movements in the commodity's price. Over time, they would update this analysis as relevant news events, weather reports and economic data releases occur, and they would adjust their trading position in the commodity accordingly.

Commodity Valuation Factors

As mentioned in the previous sections, the worth of a commodity is generally expressed in terms of the currency it is quoted in. Furthermore, this market price responds sensitively to long-term economic and interest rate cycles, as well as to shifts in policies, production efficiency and consumer demand.

Although economic theorists might postulate that commodity market price fluctuations form an essentially random walk through time, and some even use this hypothetical assumption when developing theoretical commodity option pricing models, for example, almost any cursory review of a chart of a commodity price plotted over time will probably convince you otherwise. Basically, commodity prices often show remarkable tendencies to trend in a particular direction over time, often as a response to underlying fundamental factors.

Local inflation rates can also result in persistent underlying market trends when a commodity is expressed in the affected currency, and this can affect individual commodity valuations since commodity prices tend to rise overall along with inflation. This has given certain commodities, like the precious metals for example, the reputation of being an inflation hedge for long term investors.

Furthermore, the repeatability of the aggregate behavior of large groups of humans often reflects itself in the formation of recognizable technical price patterns that set up reliable outcomes commodity traders can observe and exploit. As detailed in the previous section on technical analysis, many technical commodity traders use such patterns to forecast future commodity price movements.

Basically, if the supply and demand factors for a commodity remain fairly consistent, then its price tends to rise along with other commodities due to inflation.

Fundamental versus Technical Analysis for Trading

In terms of the point of separation between the two disciplines of technical and fundamental analysis, technicians rely primarily on market observables like price and volume data, and information derived from those factors, as they evolve over time. Fundamental analysts, on the other hand, take into account just about everything else other than those factors.

Furthermore, when considering the relative merits of focusing on economic fundamental analysis versus technical forms of market analysis many seasoned market pros note some serious issues both with performing fundamental analysis and also with its effectiveness as a technique for forecasting future commodity prices.

A discussion of some of their more common concerns and issues with using fundamental analysis to trade commodities follows.

Fundamentals Take Time

When it comes to performing an analysis to obtain a commodity price forecast, a fundamental analyst usually has to review a far greater set of information than the technical analyst.

For example, a fundamental analyst might have to look over the supply and demand factors, any relevant news and recent positioning activity as provided by the Commitment of Traders or COT report.

They might also review a slew of economic data for the country or countries where the commodity is produced and/or used, as well as take into account general economic factors like interest rates, inflation rates and growth within that commodity's sector. They might also want to look at supply and demand effects, political influences, geopolitical events, weather reports, and the prices of other relevant commodities.

Basically, the complexity of the tasks involved in performing fundamental analysis for commodities can get quite daunting. As a result, such fundamental traders can easily get left behind on market moves and stuck deep in analysis paralysis, while the technical traders may have already performed their analysis quickly and moved appropriately into the market in a much more timely fashion.

Lack of Specific Trade Recommendations

Most technical analysts have developed and follow in a disciplined way one or more clearly-defined trade plans. These sets of trading guidelines tell them valuable and objective information about what to look for, when to enter the market, and at what levels positions should be liquidated at a profit or loss.

Technical trade plans also usually incorporate money management principles that tell the trader how to size their trades, which generally depends on their risk tolerance and margin account size. Trading plans will be covered in greater detail in Chapter 9 of this book.

Unfortunately, fundamental analysts usually do not enjoy the advantage of having such clear and objective trade plans to direct their trading activities. It can be difficult for a fundamental analyst to incorporate all of the information they need to review into a specific trade recommendation with pre-defined entry and exit points.

The lack of objectivity when using fundamental analysis alone can often make the difference between a trader ultimately being successful or not. As a result, many fundamental analysts will use their techniques to forecast the overall long term trend for a commodity while using technical analysis to help them get into the market.

All News is Old News

The idea behind this issue with fundamental analysis is that any news released to the public has pretty much already been noted, analyzed and fully discounted into the market price by professional market-makers and futures exchange traders.

Basically, their intense job requires them to keep their fingers right on the pulse of the market using rapid market data services, news wires and the commodity market's own well-developed rumor-mill.

As a result, traders looking to take short term positions based on fundamentals will often be sorely frustrated to see the commodity price react to favorable news in a thoroughly counter-intuitive way by falling as the market pros "buy the rumor and sell the fact."

This happens because the market had already discounted a favorable price move based on the rumor of an event, and so when the actual event occurs, such smart traders will take profits by selling into a price rise resulting from increased anticipated demand for the commodity.

CHAPTER 7: MONEY AND RISK MANAGEMENT FOR COMMODITY TRADERS

Trading commodities successfully often has much more to do with what you avoid losing than in making big profits. When trading well by being disciplined and closely following a sound trading plan, money seems to come easily.

Nevertheless, commodity traders need to learn to take the good trades with the bad, so using basic money management suggestions like those contained in the sections below can save just about any trader money, stress and frustration.

Basic Money Management Principles

No discussion about trading seems complete without covering the basic money management principles that virtually all successful financial markets traders use and describing how to apply them when trading commodities.

This will be done in this section by explaining a series of maxims that most traders are — or should be — taught before they put actual money at risk in the markets.

- **Never risk funds you cannot afford to lose.**

Since commodities trading is gambling and not investing, you will want to avoid trading with your mortgage money or your family's food money. The pressure of placing your hard-earned funds at risk on a commodities trade might not result in the optimum trading mindset for your eventual profitably.

- **Let your profits run and cut your losses short.**

A time-tested commodity trading maxim, this saying encourages traders to let profits keep appreciating and to take losses quickly. The act of staying in a trade while a market is trending for a large part of the move can be one of the most profitable trading strategies for some. Also, taking losses quickly when you are wrong will avoid having small losses grow into much larger ones.

- **If you can't take the heat, stay out of the kitchen.**

When applied in the market, having excessive heat in your commodity trading portfolio means that you are probably trading in larger sizes than would be appropriate for the funds in your account. It might also involve some other reason that your commodities position is making you lose sleep at night. The point is that you need to feel comfortable with your commodity trading risk.

- **Avoid trading without a stop-loss.**

Because of the nature of the commodities market, price moves can sometimes be extreme and dramatic. If you neglect to protect yourself by placing a stop-loss in the market, you risk the possibility that your position may go seriously against you during an unexpected time of high volatility. This can often result in you incurring a larger eventual loss than if you had entered a stop-loss order at an appropriate level in the first place.

- **Never over-leverage your trading account.**

In practice, commodity trades can often be leveraged with a 5 to 1 ratio between the trading position you can control with any given level of funds deposited as margin, although leverage ratios can vary between brokers. Such a leverage ratio means you can control a $500 position with only $100 on deposit and that both gains and losses will be magnified by a factor of five when you employ the full ratio as a trader.

Remember to keep close track of the margin and leverage levels set by your commodities broker and work out a reasonable position-sizing strategy to manage your trading risk optimally and protect your account. Avoid overextending your commodity trading account using leverage, since it acts as a two-edged sword and can magnify trading losses as well as gains.

- **Do not give in to greed.**

Greed can get a commodity trader in plenty of trouble, such as running a winning trade into a loss, or prompting overtrading and excessive risk-taking. Another market adage goes: "Bulls make money and bears make money, but pigs get slaughtered."

Avoid trying to squeeze the last tick out of a trade since many good traders will tell you they always get out of a winning position too soon. Basically, you will never go broke taking a profit.

It also pays to remember that taking losses is a part of the trading game. As long as a commodity trader can manage risk in a disciplined way and employs prudent money management techniques, their losses will be so much less than their winning trades, that the losers will have little effect on the overall profitability of their trading business.

Why Money Management is Essential When Trading

When trading commodities or any type of asset or financial instrument, using sound money management principles considerably increases your likelihood of success over the long run.

The most profitable traders generally rely on money management techniques to ensure their objectivity and clarity when trading and to protect their account balance from a devastating loss.

Traders commonly employ some basic techniques to manage their risk, so the rest of this section will cover the importance of using money management techniques as a commodity trader and will describe some of the more popular of money management methods commonly in use by commodity traders.

Position Sizing

When developing a trading plan, a commodities trader will determine how much of their account will be put at risk for each individual trade. For example, on a $10,000 account, perhaps the trader will risk 1% on each trade. After ten consecutive losses of 1% each, the trader will still have roughly 90% of the account's value intact.

Now suppose that the trader wants to risk 5% per trade. After ten consecutive losing trades, their trading account would be left with about half of its original value and the trader may decide to go out of business.

Accordingly, an important factor when assessing and comparing commodity trading plans is the "maximum drawdown" seen with the system over recent commodity price action. This is the most substantial percentage drop from a peak to a bottom, in terms of the account's equity, seen over a certain period of time.

Stop-Loss Orders

Most successful commodities traders use stop-loss orders and enter them immediately upon initiating a commodities position. A stop-loss order consists of an order to liquidate an existing position at a worse price than the present market price.

Such an order would generally be entered at a level below the level that the position was initiated if the original position was going long. Conversely, a stop would be above the level the position was originally taken, if it was a sale. Performing this important risk-management activity will limit the trader's losses if they enter into a position that subsequently goes against them.

Trailing Stops

A useful money management technique involves using trailing stop orders that consist of entering stop-loss orders that have their level scaled upwards if the trader holds a long position that becomes profitable, in order to protect accumulated profits. Similarly, the stop-loss order levels would get scaled downward when the trader has a profitable short position.

Furthermore, if the stop losses on profitable traders are moved to the breakeven point on the trade, this common practice ensures that the trade will not show a loss, regardless of whether the market turns. Then, as the trailing-stop is scaled up or down depending on the position's direction, this will ensure that the trader continues to make and lock in profits while the favorable trend continues.

Risk Management

The importance of risk-management cannot be stressed enough, and one could make a strong case that it forms the most crucial part of a successful trading plan. Furthermore, a trader should employ risk management techniques that involve taking losses quickly and letting profits grow. This means they can have many more losing trades than winning trades and yet still be successful in the long run.

Basically, the trader benefits from taking fewer, but much more profitable trades. By the same token, the many losing trades they made involved taking relatively small losses.

Money Management Mistakes Traders Make

Money management, some experienced traders argue, takes precedence over all other considerations when it comes to trading. Because of the volatility in the commodity market, a trader without a money management component in their trading plan could be likened to a skydiver without a parachute. In the event of a string of losing trades, the trader's account will drop much like a skydiver without the benefit of a parachute to slow their fall.

A large percentage of people that begin trading in the commodity market fail mainly because of lack of discipline and poor money management. Without knowing how to deal with losing trades, many novice traders start "chasing money out the door" by committing a slew of money management mistakes and eventually losing a lot of money and even their whole initial account balance in some cases.

Some sound advice about how to manage money responsibly when trading has already been given, but it helps to know where the money management pitfalls lie so you can avoid them. What therefore follows are the some of the top money management mistakes commodity traders make and how to avoid them to help you stay in business as a trader over the long run:

1. **Not having a money management plan** – as mentioned above, without a money management component in a trading plan, the trader will not be able to weather a string of losses.

2. **Neglecting to position size trades** – a good trader will know exactly what percentage of the account will be at risk on any given trade and will not extend trading beyond the limits of the account's funding. Generally, commodities traders will risk between 1% and 5% of the trading account's value on any given trade, and by always risking the same percentage, the trader's trade size will grow along with the equity in the account.

3. **Failing to use stop-loss orders** – if a trader does not use stop-loss orders, then they better be prepared for whatever the market has in store for them. Stop-loss orders will save the trader from a loss becoming a bigger loss and are a key money management tool. In order to effectively trade with stops, the trader would do well to examine the technical indicators and place stop-loss orders accordingly, thereby maintaining an objective demeanor.

4. **Becoming emotionally involved with a position** – a serious mistake many traders make. Emotional involvement in the commodities market can be devastating to a trading account; a trader may insist on holding on to a losing trade simply because they think the market will come back. Yes, the market may come back, but when? Refusing to admit they are wrong and holding on to a losing position will affect the trader psychologically and impair their ability to trade. Emotions are best saved for one's sweetheart and not the commodities market. As the market adage states "don't marry your position."

5. **"Averaging" or doubling up on a losing position** – one of the worst mistakes a trader can make involves compounding a loser by adding to a losing position at a "better price" in the belief the market is headed the other way. In effect, the new position would be at a better price thus, averaging the price of two losers.

6. **Failure to take profits** – not taking profits once a trade has run its course can make a loser out of a winner.

7. **Trading with the rent money** – if you can't afford to lose the money you are trading with you will suffer severely in the case of a loss.

8. **Over leveraging the account** – in the commodities market you are basically trading a contract for the delivery of a large amount of a given commodity at a leveraged price which is usually a fifth or 20%. While you can make a lot of money if you are right when leveraging, you will probably be wiped out quicker if you are wrong.

9. **Letting losses run** – the saying is "let your profits run" not the other way around.

10. **Greed** – getting greedy will only get you in trouble. Greed can lead to a number of money management mistakes like overtrading and position averaging. Remember, bulls make money and bears make money but pigs get slaughtered.

Common Commodity Trading Risks

No book on getting started as a commodity trader would be complete without a discussion on the common commodity trading risks that can make your business less successful. Trading risk can be defined as the risk of incurring a substantial trading loss or allowing a prolonged trading error to erode the value of your trading account. All trading involves risk to some degree, and without risk, there would be no potential profit.

For example, volatility, or price swings, is a common commodity trading risk, but volatility is also one of the reasons that the commodity markets can be so lucrative to trade. In essence, it is due to the fact that the often-volatile natures of the various commodities markets have risk inherent in trading them that the commodity markets can provide a handsome return for those willing to take that risk in a disciplined way.

Furthermore, trading risk can be broken down into three basic categories which involve market-related risk, trading error risks that are not strictly related to market conditions and fundamental risks.

Market-Related Risks

All market risks relate to general economic conditions that affect supply and demand, the broader commodity market, and the particular commodity involved. Risk factors that affect the entire trading community interested in speculating on price changes in a particular commodity are included in this category.

Common commodity trading risks related to market conditions include:

- **High Volatility:** Strong price swings seen in fast markets can trigger the execution of stop-loss orders and may also incur order level slippage when the trade would otherwise have been profitable.

- **Directional Errors:** An error in judgment on the direction of the market that results in the trade being stopped-out at a loss.

- **Illiquidity:** A loss of liquidity can occur when markets are thin that tends to widen bid/offer spreads and can potentially render short-term trading and scalping strategies ineffective.

While directional errors seem almost inevitable, most traders can avoid the other two risks by closing out positions and avoiding trading during fast or thin markets.

Remember, market risk exists in all markets where a large number of people are trading due to the existence of a mass psychology. Market risk involves the "madness of crowds" and can be exemplified by famous market price bubbles such as "Tulipmania" and the Internet bubble in the stock market. As long as the human element persists in markets, its presence and effect on the trading of commodities cannot be overlooked.

Furthermore, human psychology and the hopes and fears of millions of market participants ultimately dictate the price action of any commodity or financial instrument. Commodities are only worth what someone will pay for them. If the humans of the world suddenly all became vegetarian, then what would happen to the price of cattle futures?

Commodity trading involves risk, so if you hear about a risk-free commodities "investment," think again. Risk and reward go together, so without taking any risk you should expect no reward.

If you do decide to trade commodities, make sure to have a good trade plan and use sound money management techniques. Above all, know what you are doing, so take the time to get educated about the commodity market and what moves it before you start to trade it.

Trading Errors

This type of risk includes all risks unrelated to market conditions and in particular, those types of trading risks which arise out of trading plan errors or other trader mistakes. The trading risks of this type do not necessarily arise from market movements and can include the following:

- Drawdown risk, which involves having an unlucky string of consecutive losing transactions that deplete a trading account to an uncomfortable level.
- Lack of discipline in following a set trading plan resulting in excessive losses.
- Losing money on price spreads and commissions as a result of overtrading.

- Failing to execute a transaction.
- Forgetting the execution of a transaction.
- Executing a transaction incorrectly, such as buying when you meant to sell.
- Failing to record a transaction.
- Failing to place a stop loss or take profit order on a transaction.
- Erroneous position sizing resulting in taking too much or too little risk on a transaction.
- Failing to diversify your commodity trading portfolio.
- Lacking a decisive attitude because of fear of losing money leading to "analysis paralysis," thereby passing up on lucrative trading opportunities.
- Excessive greed in taking profits in a timely fashion, with the possibility of making initially profitable trades turn into losers.

By avoiding this latter group of largely-unnecessary trading risks, a trader stands a much better chance of being successful. Furthermore, this can often simply be done by keeping careful trading and order records, and by adhering closely to a trading plan.

Fundamental Risks

Commodity trading carries an inherent risk due to certain fundamental factors that can vary significantly between commodities. As described in greater detail in Chapter 6 on commodity price analysis, common commodities trading risks include a variety of different types of risk that frequently depend on the particular commodity in question.

For example, risks for different commodities can be divided into:

- **Economic Risk**

    This type of risk can be ubiquitous, since everyone to some degree feels the effects of economic conditions. For example, precious metals prices can reflect economic conditions.

    If a period of disinflation and stagnant or lower prices on goods and services prevails in world markets, then precious metals prices tend to decline. If, on the other hand, overall prices of other commodities are rising in an inflationary economic environment, precious metals appreciate in tandem and often even outperform other types of investment.

- **Political Risk**

Depending on the part of the world where political upheaval takes place, commodity prices can be directly impacted. The oil-rich Middle East provides a perfect example. Oil prices in the developed world often react to the political situation in the Middle East. When war breaks out, oil prices tend to skyrocket.

Another way political events can create risk in commodities markets involves government elections. Sometimes this can present the risk of the nationalization of natural resources previously under corporate control. Recent examples include the nationalization of copper in Chile in the 1970's and oil in Venezuela in the 1990's.

- **Weather and Geological Disasters**

Weather directly affects any commodity of an agricultural nature. A bumper crop due to weather conditions optimum for growing a particular agricultural commodity will invariably make prices drop. On the other hand, an early freeze can send prices soaring.

Furthermore, an unseasonably cold winter causes higher heating oil consumption, thereby making crude oil prices rise from which heating oil is derived. The cold weather can also affect the prices of other commodities, such as wool and cotton.

Hot weather can also affect the pricing of agricultural commodities since it tends to result in drought which will affect the condition of both crops and livestock. Heat also tends to increase the consumption of electricity for air conditioning which will often make prices of coal used for the generation of electricity and other sources of energy rise.

In addition, wet weather may cause flooding due to prolonged rain that can destroy crops, and strong weather like hurricanes can disrupt the production of many commodities. Weather basically affects the pricing of many commodities, and it contributes substantially to the risk inherent in commodities trading.

In addition to the above risks, natural disasters like earthquakes, volcanic eruptions and tsunamis for example, will tend to affect prices of commodities that are produced, refined, distributed or used where the natural disaster occurred.

Commodity Trading Risks to Avoid

This section should help you distinguish between the commodity trading risks to avoid and the risks you want to be taking as a trader. When considering the trading risks to avoid, one first has to acknowledge that a trader generally has to take risks in order to earn a profit trading commodities.

Those juicy, profit-generating risks are absolutely necessary to your trading business, and they do not fall among the group of preventable risks that a trader generally wants to keep away from.

In fact, an important part of becoming a successful trader involves learning how to maintain the necessary confidence in yourself for you to continue to identify and take such risks, even after having incurred some difficult losses.

Commodity Trading Risks to Avoid – The Unnecessary Ones

Part of getting constructive experience as a trader involves learning that some potentially-costly trading risks can be rather easily circumvented by carefully managing the trading process as it unfolds. These comprise the category of unnecessary trading risks that will be addressed further in this section.

Sometimes, taking an unnecessary risk can make you an unanticipated and seemingly unlikely profit. For example, perhaps you thought you had bought when in fact you made a transactional error and actually sold, but the market declined in your favor. You were lucky to get out of that error at a profit, but it just as easily could have been a loss.

Unfortunately, you cannot count on unintentional trading errors resulting in such windfall profits every time. The trade could have resulted in a nasty and unprotected loss that could even have wiped out your trading portfolio, especially if you are a smaller margin trader. Any stop loss or take profit orders routinely entered to protect the intended position could instead have magnified the problem given the incorrectly entered trade.

Accordingly, doing what you can to avoid such risky errors and generally directing your risk-taking toward trades that are intentional, have good risk/reward ratios, and accurately reflect your market view will be more likely to keep you in business as a trader over the long run.

Primary Unnecessary Trading Risks

Specifically, some potentially-costly commodity trading risks that you want to be aware of and actively seek to avoid when trading include the following:

1. **Loss of Trading Discipline**

This risk occurs when a trader fails to follow the trade plan they have set up for themselves in a disciplined manner. Since the trade plan was designed to keep them within safe trading parameters, the risk of circumventing it is unknown and potentially large. Plan your trade and trade your plan should be your mantra.

2. **Overtrading**

Some commodity traders, especially novices, find executing trades fun and exciting. As a result, they display a tendency to start to trade without a plan or they might trade too often, perhaps taking an excessive number of trades that lack good risk/reward ratios. If such traders do manage to make profits, much of what they earn tends to get eaten up by spreads and commissions. The pros know that it is generally better for the long-term health of their trading business to learn to "sit on their hands" and wait for the good trades to show up than to trade too much.

3. **Analysis Paralysis**

Some traders succumb to "analysis paralysis" as they get overwhelmed with all of the fundamental information and technical indicators they could be looking at when making a trading decision and therefore fail to act in time to take what would have been a winning trade. While one should definitely avoid overtrading, you will still need to trade sometimes to make money as a commodity trader.

If you find yourself watching screens all day without ever trading, then perhaps you need to lower your risk/reward standards and jump into the market to get your feet wet. Practice making and execute trading decisions quickly and incorporate that idea into your trade plan since the commodity markets wait for no one.

Other Unnecessary Trading Risks to Avoid

Other unnecessary risks to avoid when trading commodities that generally indicate a lack of adherence to your trade plan might include the following five errors:

1. Failing to pull the trigger
2. Jumping the gun
3. Not taking timely profits
4. Moving or pulling stops
5. Entering low probability trades.

Finally, keep careful records of your commodity trades, and do your best to confirm each and every transaction you make in order to avoid potentially-costly transactional errors. The same degree of attention and care needs to go into placing the orders you need to have to protect your profits and limit your losses.

While you cannot control the market, you can certainly exercise power over your own behavior. That alone is what often differentiates the experienced trader from the novice and the winner from the loser.

CHAPTER 8: COMMODITY TRADER PSYCHOLOGY

When it comes to trading any financial market, the unique psychological makeup you bring to the endeavor — combined with your mindset when actually trading — can have a very substantial impact on your success and enjoyment of trading.

This chapter will cover some of the basic things you need to know about the psychology of trading so that you can start optimizing your chances for success by thinking and behaving in ways that tend to support profitability as a trader.

Why Psychology is so Important to Commodity Traders

Most traders who wish to stay in business over the long term generally approach their work using a trading plan which they expect to follow closely. Nevertheless, to keep to a trading plan in a disciplined way is not as easy as you might initially think.

Regardless of how effective a trading system might be in theory, the truth remains that a system is only as good as how much discipline the trader using it maintains during its implementation in practice. If the trader only follows their trading system partially, then they will only obtain partial results that will probably not be the results they want.

Nevertheless, some traders permit some flexibility to enter their trading systems. Often, this might come into plan when taking profits, for example. Having this type of flexibility and being able to exercise judgment can even be a key element in such traders' overall success.

The rest of this section will discuss the importance of psychology in the field of commodity trading and how successful traders use psychology to maximize profits.

Psychology and Trading

When trading, a trader's mindset and psychology often determines whether they will eventually be profitable. Successful traders usually know that emotions can hurt their ability to approaching their work objectively and that trading errors made due to emotions can even cost them their business.

As they participate in the trading process, a trader can become their own worst enemy if they allow emotions to have any part in determining the outcome of their trades. In fact, studies have shown that a trader's psychological approach or mindset can account for up to 80% of what makes a trader successful.

Reacting to Adversity

For example, knowing how they react in adverse trading situations gives an experienced trader an advantage over a novice trader or a person who has no experience in the field whatsoever.

Consider the case of a trader that has initiated a position which immediately shows a loss. They now have two options:

1. Keep the trade as an "investment" and wait for the market to go the other way.

2. Liquidate the trade immediately and take a small loss.

A seasoned trader will probably either liquidate the losing trade immediately, or perhaps they might hold the trade for a short period until they were sure the market had failed to turn around, maintaining either a stop loss level in the market or in their heads.

A trader with less experience, on the other hand, can often tend to hold the trade without a time or price limit, hoping that the market might turn in order to recover their loss.

The Emotions of Fear, Hope and Greed

The above example illustrates two basic emotions at play in trading psychology: fear and hope. The seasoned trader justifiably fears losing more money and quickly liquidates the position. In this case, they use the emotion of fear appropriately to cut losses and keep them from increasing to an uncomfortable level.

On the other hand, the novice trader relies on their hopeful emotions, rather than on common sense and reason, in thinking the market might turn around. In effect, this allows losses on the trade to grow as the market continues going against the position.

Another key emotion which finds ample expression in the world of trading is greed. This can be defined as the desire to acquire more than you need or deserve. When trading, giving into greed can have serious consequences, such as failing to take profits when appropriate. This error can often cause a trader to turn an initially profitable trade into a disappointing loss.

Basically, the importance of psychology when operating in the commodity market, and virtually any market for that matter, cannot be overstated. Mass psychology is responsible for both economic bubbles, where greed drives a market to unsupportable highs, as well as economic depressions, where fear causes exaggerated selling pressure. A good trader can learn to take advantage of both opportunities by managing their emotions when trading.

The Trading Animal Farm Analogy

It can sometimes help traders understand their own psychology and that of other market operators by drawing an analogy between trader behavior and that of certain animals.

As noted in the previous chapter, an anonymous stock market adage goes, "Bulls make money, bears make money, but pigs get slaughtered." Apparently, this warning was originally intended to remind stock traders to avoid the emotional pitfall of greediness, but it also applies very well to those looking to trade any market successfully.

To take this analogy a bit further, what can be referred to as a market's "animal farm" consists of traders who tend to conform emotionally to one or more of the classic animal personalities listed below.

The Bulls

Traders who are bulls or bullish on a particular market tend to charge ahead as they optimistically think the price for that asset is going up, up, up! As a result of their positive perspective, they will take a long position in the asset.

For example, they might believe that prospects for a particular commodity look great or are due to improve significantly relative to those observed for another related commodity.

In addition, perhaps interest or inflation rates also favor the underlying commodity market, so traders long a diverse portfolio of commodities may expect to achieve gains on their positions over the long term, which is a particularly popular strategy for precious metal traders.

Nevertheless, sometimes exchange traded futures markets do close down trading in a particular commodity when its price rises to a certain limit in order to prevent disruptive market spikes and bubbles from forming. Accordingly, even strong bulls need to remember that the commodity market has a tendency to overdo things sometimes and such excessively-directional bullish optimism can often lead to the resulting bubble bursting sharply as the market moves "up the stairs, but down the escalator" as the old market saying goes.

The Bears

This brings us to the bears. Bears can be grumpy creatures whose sour view on the market gives them pretty much the opposite take to the charging bulls. Accordingly, traders who are bears or bearish on a particular commodity pessimistically think the price for that commodity is going a good way down, and so they will take a short position in the commodity.

Unlike in the stock market, where stocks can only be sold short on an uptick on many exchanges, commodity traders can typically short any commodity whenever they can find another market participant they can trade with willing to show an acceptable bid price. Nevertheless, sometimes exchange traded futures markets do close down trading in a particular commodity when its price falls to a certain limit in order to prevent market crashes.

Bears might take a short trade if they think that production of a particular commodity may rise significantly or its market demand prospects are likely to worsen in future. This may seem justified if the price is therefore seen as falling beyond that of the underlying often-upwards trend due to inflation.

Like bulls with their excessive optimism, bears should remember that no downward trend lasts forever, so they need to be flexible enough as commodity traders to realize when the market has turned to the upside.

Interestingly, while bulls and bears are perhaps the best-known animals that commodity traders tend to resemble as they position themselves in their market, they are not the only ones. This is where the proverbial farm comes in.

The Sheep and the Chickens

The next animals in the commodity market barnyard are the sheep and the chickens. Each of these trading animals fails to make money trading commodities because they are both too afraid to take a position, although for slightly different reasons.

The sheepish trader is just too shy to try something new, while the chicken trader is afraid of getting killed when they enter the market. Together, they just sit on the proverbial sidelines, waiting for the perfect trade, which naturally never comes.

Basically, any decent commodity trader has to be willing to lose some money in order to eventually come out a winner; neither can they expect to win if they continually override their trade plan and fail to pull the trigger when their plan signals a trade.

Taking no risk means receiving no reward, so these self-sidelined traders might just break even after allowing their fear to kill their commodity trading business while they wasted plenty of their valuable time watching screens.

The Pigs

As referred to in the well-known saying at the beginning of this chapter, the next commodity market trading animal is the pig. This trading beast tends to succumb to greed and so they refuse to take profits on winning positions when appropriate, as they try to squeeze a bit more money out of the market.

Instead of taking their gains and living to trade again, they might even make the classic trading mistake of allowing their initially winning trade to turn into a losing one that costs them money. Eventually, allowing their greed to rule their trading will lead to the slaughter of the pig's trading portfolio.

Maybe no one ever went broke taking a profit, but plenty of piggish commodity traders have gone broke by failing to take one. Pigs also tend to take substantial risks boldly and without doing their homework in impatient attempts to make big, quick profits trading commodities. Unfortunately, they often end up killing their trading business in the process.

Sure, both bulls can make money and bears can make money as the pendulum of a commodity's equilibrium price swings to and fro. Even the chickens might be able to peck a few grains out of the market as the other trading animals pick up profits from the greedy losing pigs.

So, after reading this section, ask yourself what kind of commodity trading animals will you avoid being?

Emotions Commonly Experienced When Trading Commodities

Few experiences can make a person feel their emotions more intensely than trading an account with their own money in the commodity market. Trading can make a person feel on top of the world when making profits but severely depressed when watching their trading account begin to evaporate into thin air.

This section will cover what emotions traders frequently experience and what this can imply for those interested in trading the commodity market successfully.

Trading as a Business

Anyone who has ever run a business will tell you that emotions and business do not mix well. Trading the commodity market has many similarities to running a business, mainly because people who participate in trading do so to make money, just like most people aim to do with their businesses.

Nevertheless, because of the immediacy of gains and losses in the commodity market, people tend to get emotional much more easily than in other types of businesses. Even with the best laid plans, people often tend to break the rules when emotions take over, even if they have made those rules themselves.

Emotions Experienced When Trading

A list of the most common emotions that traders experience when trading and what impact these emotions may have on the trader's account are outlined below:

- **Fear** – one of the all-time market drivers. Nobody trading in the market likes to lose money and fear of losing can have repercussions on both individual traders and the market in general as fear will make markets drop faster and further than any other market emotion. Fear also impedes traders from taking action when necessary and leaves some traders holding losing positions much longer than appropriate, magnifying losses.

- **Greed** – Another major factor driving the markets. Many people do not even realize how greedy they have been conditioned by society and are surprised once they start trading. Greed can be very dangerous to a trader. An old market saying goes "bulls and bears make money but pigs get slaughtered."

- **Hope** – An important emotion that can affect traders' behavior considerably. Hope is generally felt after a trader has taken a trade which subsequently goes against them. In this case, the trader often hopes the market will turn around and make the losing trade profitable. Unfortunately, hope has no basis in reality and can only impair the trader from trading effectively and taking losses promptly to protect their portfolio. Fear of losing more money is a more appropriate emotion in this instance, and the trader should give up hope and just liquidate the position according to their plan.

- **Excitement** – Trading the commodity market can be exciting, especially when riding on a wave of winning trades. Nevertheless, such excitement can lead to a number of trading pitfalls that include overtrading and carelessness. Many such overly-excited traders have been surprised to find their account with a net loss at the end of a busy trading day after commissions and/or spreads have eaten away any profits.

- **Depression** – An emotion that a trader often feels after a string of losing trades, especially if the losses resulted from them not being disciplined. An often-crippling emotion when trading, depression finds better expression when left outside of the trading arena. Most traders stop trading if they find it makes them depressed.

- **Anger** – A common emotion experienced when a trader fails to take a profit and ends up running the trade into a loss. Also seen when a trader makes a losing trade and fails to put in a stop-loss, thus digging themselves deeper into the hole.

Basically, emotional reactions really have their proper place within relationships and not when it comes to trading the commodity market. Remember, if trading is going to be your business, you need to treat it like one.

How Emotions Can Impact Your Commodity Trading Profitability

When trading in the commodity market for your own account, your emotions and how you manage them can become the single most challenging issue facing both new and seasoned traders alike.

Basically, dealing with the intense emotions generated when trading can be daunting to anyone, and so knowing how to cope with how you feel after an unsuccessful trade is as important as knowing when to get in and out of the market.

Furthermore, for most successful commodity traders, having learned how to effectively deal with their emotions represents a key element of their success. Attaining mastery over your emotions therefore forms a main part of the ideal trading mindset.

The rest of this section will explain how emotions can directly affect the profitability of a commodity trader, and how seasoned commodity traders manage their emotions when trading.

Fear

As one of the most elemental human emotions and therefore a key factor in trading any market, fear can either be useful or detrimental, depending on the trader's mindset. In its most useful sense, fear works as a defense mechanism as in the "fight or flight" instinct shared by virtually all higher beings.

When trading markets, fear can affect a person in a number of ways and often finds expression as:

- Fear of failure.
- Fear of missing a trade or missing out on a move.
- The fear of losing profits already earned.
- The fear of impending doom or loss.

While fear can spur a trader to cut losses before they get bigger, the emotion can also impact a trader by rendering them ineffective as they watch losses grow. Such an experience can make the trader reluctant to continue trading and thus result in them missing other potentially-profitable trading opportunities.

Greed

The fictional Gordon Gekko character from the 1986 movie "Wall Street" was perhaps best known for the famous line: "Greed is good." Without debating that controversial point, greed nevertheless constitutes a major part of the commodity market's participants' emotional make-up. It can also affect traders in ways that many only discover after they begin trading.

Some of the ways in which greed directly affects traders follow:

- **Failure to Take Profits** – Some traders manifest greed by not taking profits according to their set trading plan. Instead, the trader might hold out for a little extra money, or perhaps see their losses erode as the market turns.

- **Overtrading** – traders often make this mistake in a hurried attempt to make money instead of patiently waiting for optimum trading opportunities.

- **Taking Profits Too Early** – When traders realize their gains ahead of the levels that their trading plan indicates, this often results in a smaller profit than if the original plan was followed. Remember to let your profits run.

- **Taking Excessive Risks** – Greed can also manifest by a trader taking excessive risks in an attempt to make large profits fast. This generally leads to disaster as encapsulated by the old market saying that goes: "Bulls make money, bears make money, but pigs get slaughtered."

Hope

After the serious impact of fear and greed, hope often gets overlooked. Nevertheless, the emotion still manifests and affects traders in decidedly unprofitable ways. In general, hope arises when a trader has a losing trade and continues feeling that they are still on the right side of the market.

A trader in this situation often hopes that the market will come back, but yet this may never occur, prompting the currently losing trade to become an even bigger loser. Eventually, the trader might wind up taking a much larger loss than if they had put in a stop-loss and gotten out right after incurring the initial loss.

Not only do such experiences result in losses, but having such an experience will often psychologically scar the trader by shaking their self-confidence.

Overcoming Emotions When Trading

Overall, emotions need expression when trading, but they cannot be relied upon to make prudent trading decisions and can adversely affect your trading profitability.

As an alternative, maintaining strict adherence to a proven trading plan can provide an excellent defense against giving in to emotions experienced while trading.

Managing Emotions When Commodity Trading

Trading the commodity markets differs from most fields of endeavor in that even the most profitable and efficient trading systems can be sabotaged by the human element. The trader that gets caught up in an emotional whirlwind while trading usually only has a limited time in the business and probably not a pleasant one at that.

Emotions are a natural human response, but every trader needs to learn to manage their emotions in order to be successful. Furthermore, even if a trading system has been proven to work under all market conditions, the system can only be as good as the person implementing it.

Accordingly, if a lack of discipline exists in the trader's approach, it really does not matter how well their system would otherwise perform.

The Psychology of Losing Trades: Cut Losses Short

Trading the commodity market successfully often requires behavior that goes contrary to normal human psychology. For example, consider the situation in which a novice trader has made a losing trade but still stubbornly thinks the market is wrong and they are correct. As a result, they decide to hold the trade in the hope that the market will change its direction and eventually allow the trade to return to profitability.

The novice trader's reaction approaches the normal psychological reaction that just about any optimistic person would have in the same situation. Still, it is always better to be right than optimistic when it comes to trading commodities, and as the market saying goes, "Cut your losses short."

Furthermore, this novice trader may have to wait a long time for the market to turn, if it ever does. They may also have to suffer unpleasant margin calls due to the erosion of their trading account in the meantime. This could serious curtail their ability to take full advantage of future moves they would have called correctly.

In this case, this trader would do much better by replacing the optimistic hope of the market reversing, with the fear of losing more money that has far greater significance when it comes to staying in business as a trader.

Unfortunately, most novice traders rely too much on hope than is appropriate when trading, making it considerably more difficult for them to be effective and successful at the endeavor in the long run.

The Psychology of Winning Trades: Let Profits Run

Alternatively, if a novice trader has a trade that immediately shows a profit, the normal psychological reaction might be to liquidate the trade immediately after the profit arises, thereby ensuring a gain. This makes some sense since "No one ever went broke taking a profit", as the old saying goes.

Nevertheless, this saying actually contains a hidden warning about how taking losses could clear out your trading account, rather than offering a suggestion to take a profit as soon as you see one. Instead, the preferable market trading maxim to remember when dealing with winning positions recommends, "Let your profits run."

More experienced traders often allow their profits to expand appropriately by entering trailing stop-loss orders at increasingly tighter levels as the market moves in their direction. This technique helps ensure that the trade gets liquidated close to the best possible profit-taking level before the market reverses, not merely at the first sign of a profit.

The Mindset of a Successful Commodity Trader

All truly successful traders share certain characteristics, regardless of what market they are trading or what trading system they are using. One such attribute is their mindset. In this case, a trading mindset refers to the state of mind of the trader when engaged in their trading activities.

The rest of this section will discuss how maintaining a favorable mindset for success, including working from a pre-determined trading plan and following its rules closely, usually notably increases a commodity trader's profitability.

Elements for a Successful Trading Mindset

In order to achieve consistent success in commodity trading, most experts consider two elements of utmost importance:

1. **Trading Plan** – This is a written set of strategic guidelines for a trader to follow that covers things like how and when trading will take place. Provided that it is well-defined and profitable, the trade plan need not be complicated. In fact, many of the best trading plans are kept simple in order to be easy to follow.

2. **Discipline** – Involves the trader having the willpower to follow their plan. Many traders find this element the most challenging, because emotions often get in the way and incite a trader to break their own rules. In essence, having rules and sticking to them become two entirely different matters when trading.

Furthermore, to develop a constructive trading mindset, a novice trader must be aware that trading can, and usually does, highlight character issues that my not even have entered the trader's awareness beforehand. These issues, such as feelings of unworthiness, can manifest unconsciously as counterproductive behavior during the trading process, thereby causing the trader to lose money.

Have a Trading Plan

Having a solid trading plan, while very important, really only consists of half of the game. Implementing the plan and having the discipline to follow one's own rules becomes the real crux of the biscuit.

Several common errors that traders make while executing a trading plan include:

- Letting greed influence trading decisions and not exiting trades according to the trading plan.
- Allowing fear to impede taking action when the trading plan indicates taking a position.
- Using too much leverage resulting in taking more risk than necessary when trading.

- Enjoying the trading process a bit too much and losing money by overtrading.
- Making costly errors through carelessness in executing trades and placing orders.

All of the above mistakes reflect to some degree the trader's underlying psychological makeup. Furthermore, they can include emotional responses that may not have arisen had the person not started trading.

The mindset of a successful trader will have worked out suitable responses to many, if not all, of these issues and therefore stays more focused on implementing the trading plan rigorously.

Keep a Trade Journal

Keeping a journal which tracks not only every trade, but the emotions generated by each trade can prove invaluable in becoming a successful trader. Such a journal might have the trader's trading plan at the beginning as a reminder to keep to it. It also will ideally detail their emotional responses to both winning and losing trades, with a special emphasis on the latter.

In essence, the mindset of a successful commodity trader keeps centered on trading according to their well-defined trading plan and minimizing any emotional responses to their trading activities. This helps ensure that the trader will be as objective as possible and will therefore find their emotions less distracting.

Finally, many traders find that studying the mindset and psychology of other successful traders can prove extremely helpful. Learning from the mistakes that others have already made can save any trader both money and frustration.

Developing an Ideal Commodity Trading Mentality

Developing an ideal commodity trading mentality does not have to be difficult. As long as a trader is willing to make a commitment to being disciplined in adhering to a well-defined trading plan, achieving the mindset of a successful trader falls well within the reach of all traders.

This section covers the principles and general steps involved in developing an optimum commodity trading mentality that will help virtually any trader start out on the right foot or get back on track to success.

Good Traders Have a Plan

Of course, to achieve this mindset goal, finding or developing a trading plan would be the first order of business. Trading systems generally have their basis in technical analysis. For example, they might use technical indicators such as Relative Strength Indicators and moving averages to generate buy and sell signals on which to initiate trading positions.

The Internet provides a number of resources for learning about technical analysis, as well as entire online trading platforms with an impressive array of technical indicators and charting software. Many of these trading platforms have programmable features that can assist a trader in developing and automating their own trading system.

Items to Include in a Trading Plan

A list of four items that would be useful to include in a trading plan to enhance your trading mindset follow:

1. Pre-determined entry points to initiate trades.

2. Levels for stop-loss orders to manage risk after establishing a losing trading position.

3. Levels for take-profit orders to lock in gains after establishing a winning trading position.

4. Position-sizing specifications related to the size of the account and your risk tolerance.

Incorporate Trading Plan Flexibility

For the trading plan to have an optimum level of effectiveness in generating profits, incorporating a certain amount of flexibility in it generally allows for specific exceptions, especially with respect to profit-taking.

This allows a trader to take advantage of unforeseen circumstances and opportunities, without losing their resolve to manage risk effectively on unprofitable trades.

Strengthen Confidence in Your Trading System and Yourself

In order to achieve the ideal commodity trading mentality, it can really help to build confidence in your system by seeing its trading performance under back-testing and demo trading conditions. This process also allows you to make any necessary modifications to your system before placing your hard-earned money on the line.

Your success when practice or demo trading will also give you a good idea if you already have the strategic and disciplined commodity trading mentality necessary to become a successful trader. Also, any success you had will probably also give you greater confidence when placing actual funds at risk.

Furthermore, having confidence in an objective trading plan or strategy by having tested it makes a trader much more likely to execute it with the required discipline. This allows the trader to achieve an optimum trading mentality, and helps makes trading a much less emotional endeavor.

Achieving a Successful Trading Mindset

Generally, achieving the ideal mindset for trading the commodity markets boils down to having three things in place well before live trading begins:

1. A reliably-profitable and tested trading system.

2. The self-confidence to take action when called for.

3. A sound money management component in the trading system.

These three elements, while not being a guarantee of profitability, will tend to make trading much less difficult and more manageable on an emotional level.

Also, by having solutions already worked out in their trade plan well before problems arise, a trader can stay much more in tune with the market and thereby achieve a level of success that may surprise even them.

CHAPTER 9: COMMODITY TRADING AS A BUSINESS

Many new commodity traders who just jump into the market often find it necessary to stop trading for a while in order to figure out what went wrong and why they did not have the success they initially anticipated.

Planning in advance how you intend to run your trading business can be a helpful process to avoid such a potentially painful lesson. Taking the time for such forethought will also start your process of becoming more strategic as a trader, which should greatly improve your chances of success.

Developing a Commodity Trading Business Plan

One of the best ways to start developing a plan for your business is to write down a comprehensive guide for you to follow when managing your trading activities.

Doing so can really help you understand your goals when participating in commodity trading and can also provide a detailed business plan laying out how you intend to achieve them both to yourself and potentially interested investors in your trading business.

This section discusses how to develop a business plan to increase your chances of profitability when trading commodities.

Writing a Successful Trading Business Plan

Seven suggested steps that you can go through sequentially to develop such a trade plan are as follows:

- **Step 1: Set Commodity Trading Goals**
  Describe in detail why you want to start trading commodities, what needs you hope to fulfill by doing so, and how achieving that goal will make you feel.

- **Step 2: Determine Financial Status and Objectives**
  List how much money you have to fund your trading portfolio with, what sort of income you require or expect from your trading activities and over what time frame, and what that will translate to in terms of a percentage increase in your trading portfolio's capitalization over a suitable time frame.

- **Step 3: Trading Psychology**
  Explain your overall psychology when trading, including such items as: how you analyze market movements, on what time frames you prefer to trade, how you feel under a normal range of trading events, and how you plan on managing your emotions while trading.

- **Step 4: Choice of Trade Strategy**
  Discuss the trading strategies that you intend to use, why you selected them, when you are going to use them and what commodities you intend to trade with each strategy.

- **Step 5: Trade Strategy Details**
  For each strategy you employ, describe first how you will enter the market. Then discuss under what circumstances you will liquidate the position, including how you will set stop loss and take profit orders.

- **Step 6: Money Management**
  Provide your money management intentions, including how you will limit risk on each trade and on your account overall. This might include limiting losses incurred in particular time frames, as well as the number of consecutive losing trades or losing days. This section would also describe what you will do if any of these risk limits are met.

- **Step 7: Demo Testing and Live Trading Plan**
  Cover how you will go about demo trading your trade plan, and under what circumstances you will stop testing it, and either scrap the plan or commence live trading using it. Also discuss how you

will begin subjecting your trade plan to testing using a live trading environment in terms of how much of your portfolio you are willing to place at risk initially, and how you might go about increasing that if the plan trades successfully.

Why Develop a Commodity Trade Plan?

Putting together a commodity trading plan makes sense for virtually any but the most casual and uncommitted trader. By following the above steps to develop a comprehensive commodity trading plan, you should gain a greater understanding of your motives and intentions when trading.

You will also start to become far more strategic about your trading activities. That progress alone can substantially improve your chances of becoming a more profitable commodity trader when you next decide to place funds at risk.

Plan Your Trades and Trade Your Plan

A very significant percentage of commodity traders fail to make money when they first start out trading. Some of these people just take their losses and quit trading, while the more persistent commodity traders will often take the time to learn what they did wrong so that they can be more confident about moving back into the market.

One of the ways to develop this confidence is to create a trade plan that describes in detail the circumstances surrounding your trading activities and also details exactly how you intend to execute your trading strategy and manage your account.

You will also want to discipline yourself to properly test your plan, and if the test succeeds, you will then need to execute this trade plan faithfully. In essence, this process is what seasoned traders are referring to when they say: "Plan your trades and trade your plan."

Basically, the advantages of having a trade plan and sticking to it when trading commodities are numerous, so this section will cover that topic and describe the trade planning process in greater detail.

How to Plan Your Trades

The first step toward greater success in trading commodities will often be to take the time to write down a detailed plan for how you intend to run your trading business, including how you enter and exit trades.

Creating such a plan will often include taking the following key steps to:

1. Set your commodity trading goals
2. Determine your financial status and objectives
3. Explain your trading psychology
4. Identify your choice of trading strategy
5. Provide trade strategy details
6. Clarify how you will perform money and risk management
7. State how you intend to demo test your strategy and then start trading your plan in a live account.

Before you make your first commodity trade or another trade, it really makes sense to take some time to think about your trade plan and put your thoughts on paper.

Trading Your Plan

Once you have developed and tested a workable trade plan, the next step is to implement it. Unfortunately, this part of the process can present considerable difficulty to traders that do not have the discipline to keep to their plan.

Such a loss of discipline might arise if the trader lacks confidence in themselves or their trade plan. It might also happen if the trader becomes overwhelmed with their emotions when trading and allows their own fear, greed or hope to direct their trading activities instead of their trade plan.

While the market sometimes gives such traders lucky breaks, unfortunately, allowing emotions to rule when trading is far more often a recipe for financial disaster.

Advantages of Having a Trade Plan

As you work though the steps toward creating a trade plan detailed in the earlier section, you will gradually be forming a commodity trading plan that will reflect your needs, desires and risk appetite.

Furthermore, you will obtain a considerably greater picture of what motivates you to trade and exactly what you intend to do when trading and under what circumstances.

Going through this relatively simple process can significantly advance you toward the goal of becoming a profitable commodity trader. It will also provide a considerably sounder basis for having confidence in your trading choices when you next start trading commodities.

How a Commodity Trade Plan Can Help Keep Emotions in Check

Emotions that arise when trading can be the downfall of any trader unprepared for their potential impact. Developing a commodity trading plan to manage such emotions can be the key to trading commodities successfully.

This section reviews the emotions experienced when trading commodities and describes the advantages that having a commodity trading plan can provide for managing them more effectively.

Common Emotional Responses Experienced When Trading

When trading an immediately profitable position, human nature leads many novice v traders to take the profit from the trade quickly. This allows them to avoid the fear of losing money and gives the trader instant gratification.

Nevertheless, if the market continues rising, the trader will usually become emotionally frustrated at having taken such a small profit instead of holding out for the higher return they might think they really deserved. Basically, taking small profits and letting losses run large is going to drain such traders' accounts far too quickly.

While the two scenarios above illustrate how normal human emotions can be detrimental to the trading process, subsequent action based on emotional reactions can make matters considerably worse. For example, inexperienced traders have a tendency to get caught up in their emotions and the fun of trading, rather than "sitting on their hands" and waiting for good trading opportunities like the more seasoned trading pros have learned to do.

This causes the novices to start to "overtrade," by taking on commodity positions with poor risk/reward ratios and trading excessively. Often, this means a net loss that is further compounded by market spreads and commissions. Although overtrading sometimes results in a pleasantly profitable surprise, it far more often leads to disaster for the trader's account.

Advantages of Managing Emotions with a Trade Plan

Many people have found out the hard way that, when it comes to trading, emotions should be controlled at the very least, and in most cases completely avoided in the decision-making process. The vast majority of successful traders develop a technical system which they incorporate into a commodity trading plan to trade the market and maintain a strictly-disciplined mindset with which to approach their trading activities.

In doing so, they avoid the pitfalls of overtrading, early profit-taking and holding onto losing positions. Furthermore, they generally end up sticking to their trading rules and managing their trading account's risk with as little emotional involvement as possible.

Emotion and trading make strange bedfellows and most seasoned traders recommend being as impersonal as possible when it comes to trading. Avoid marrying a position, have a way to determine when you are wrong and know in advance what appropriate protective actions are needed to save your portfolio from further losses.

Also, stubbornness in trading the markets has been the cause of countless serious losses, and it can be a very easy mistake to avoid if you are well aware of the severity of its risk. By developing and strictly following a commodity trade plan with a profitable track record that can be executed without much discretion, you will place yourself firmly on the right path to becoming a successful trader.

When to Make a Commodity Trade Plan

Ideally, developing a trade plan to help manage emotions would happen before you even make your first trade. Nevertheless, if you have already been trading for a while, but have not yet considered this type of risk or written down a trading business plan, you can still derive considerable benefits from doing so even now.

Basically, producing a business plan will not only assist you in controlling emotions that arise when trading, but it will also help you to review and solidify your personal trading business activities and goals. Also, if the plan looks good, you might even be able to use it to find new investors to trade for!

Business Risk Considerations When Trading Commodities

Hopefully, by now you have either formulated a trading plan or resolved to do so before stepping back into the commodity markets. Still, while many novice traders and even some experienced traders focus largely on mitigating trading risks, another important type of risk traders need to be aware of and evaluate when reviewing their trading activities is business risk. This can be defined as the risk that your business will fail to have enough funds to cover its costs.

Commodity traders need to be just as vigilant about managing business risk as they are about making trading gains since it involves doing what is necessary to stay in the trading business long term. This often means taking a closer look at your trading process from a risk versus reward perspective.

This rest of this section will covers some of the primary business risk-related issues involved in trading commodities that you should be aware of and have a plan for how to deal with them.

Business Risk/Reward Analysis

Performing a risk/reward analysis usually involves taking a reasonably objective assessment in terms of size, timing and likelihood of any risks the business might encounter.

It also involves considering what sort of rewards can reasonably be expected to result from your trading activities and to what size and over what time frame you project them to accumulate.

Also, since some risks are more probable than others, they can be weighted in a risk analysis according to their probability of occurrence, and then multiplied by the potential size of risk or loss involved.

Assessing Business Risk

Specific examples of business risks which traders can encounter, organized in two basic risk categories, appear below.

1. Financial Risks:

When trading, business risk often stems from financial risk that is related to the size and reliability of any debt being serviced so that you can stay in business trading. Business risks to traders can involve the financial risks such as:

- Losing more money trading than you can afford to.
- Displeasing your employer, domestic or business partner by spending time engaged in trading, and who then insist that you stop trading.
- Inadequate or negative returns from your trading activities that induces your investors or partners to withdraw their financial backing from your trading business.
- Having margin calls in excess of your ability to cover them due to an unfavorable market movement.
- Needing to pay interest on trading loans in excess of you can afford.

2. **Economic Risks:**

Economic risk presents another form of business risk which depends on the general regulatory and economic climate that can impact your business as a trader. The following economic risks can be encountered by traders:

- You can no longer trade because new regulations exclude you.
- Trading amounts, spreads or fees exceed what you need to continue to trade profitably.
- The tax code changes in a way that negatively impacts your trading business.
- You are unable to obtain items needed for your success due to insufficient funds or education. For traders, such things might include:
    - trading platforms
    - technical analysis systems
    - account management facilities
    - access to live news and quotes
    - trader mentoring
    - courses on trading, technical analysis and money management techniques.

Advantages of Business Risk Analysis

Assessing business risk by considering what financial and economic risks your trading business might face, in addition to performing a quantified risk/reward analysis is well worth doing and could make the difference between success and failure as a trader.

Also, such a risk analysis can be added to your trading business plan to increase its scope and broaden its perspective both for yourself and for any potential investors you might hope to attract.

CHAPTER 10: PARTING ADVICE FOR TRADERS

No introductory book about commodity trading would be complete without offering a summary and a little friendly advice because, while the mechanics of trading commodities remain relatively simple, trading commodities profitably has never been especially easy.

The basic fact remains that most inexperienced individuals tend to lose money when trading commodities, especially when they start to resemble the less successful stereotypes among the market "animal farm" on an emotional level, as was discussed earlier in this book.

That certainly does not mean that you will also lose money in commodity trading, and you might even be lucky enough to make your next fortune speculating in the commodity markets!

Nevertheless, the humbling fact remains that the commodity markets have a lot more losing participants than winners, so that means you need to start smart when it comes to your commodity trading in order to give yourself the best chances of success.

The following section will summarize many of the techniques and concepts presented earlier in this book in order to give you a clear path toward optimizing your behavior as a trader in order to produce consistent profits in your commodity trading business.

Optimizing Commodity Trading Profits

As you may have heard, trading in the commodity market can be extremely lucrative, especially for those with the proper knowledge of market analysis tools and money management strategies that have been described in previous chapters combined with the right mindset and necessary discipline required to use them.

Furthermore, basic technical analysis tools incorporated into a trading plan will generally give the trader clear signals for entering and exiting the market with a profit. The key to successful trading is in keeping that profit.

Optimizing profits in commodity trading can be dependent on the trader's particular trading style. For example, a day trader could optimize their profits by simply holding the winning trade for a slightly longer period during that day's trading session. A swing trader might use a trailing stop loss order on a successful trading position, to ensure their profit does not turn into a loss.

While trading style may have a bearing on how a trader might maximize their profits, some methods for enhancing profits are not specific to a trader's style, but can instead be applied to all trading styles to some degree. These techniques have to do with risk management and follow up strategies, which not only enhance a trader's profit but also decrease risk significantly.

This section will put together a number of the strategies and techniques introduced in previous sections with the goal of helping you to optimize your commodity trading profits.

Risk Management's Role in Maximizing Profits

Basically, the main focus of a commodity trader once they have a profitable position is to manage risk. The first risk is that of losing the profit already made by holding the position too long and thereby incurring additional risk. Risk management generally represents a key component in most successful trader's trading plans and is one of the most important elements to optimizing commodity trading profits.

Unfortunately, most novice and many experienced traders do not give risk management the respect it deserves. A good risk management component to a trading plan can make the difference between experiencing a casual minor loss and blowing out your trading account.

The risk management part of a trading plan can be as important to the trader — and should be as strictly adhered to — as the selection of entry and exit points for initiating and liquidating positions. Risk management rules ideally are clearly defined in the plan, and the trader should be fully aware of what they stand to lose, as well as having some concrete idea about when to get out on every position.

In order to preserve capital and to trade profitably, a trader's risk management rules ideally become second nature. To optimize profits, profitable trades must first be made. Risk management tools which can be used to directly optimize profits are discussed in the following sections.

Appropriate Position Sizing is Essential

Regardless of the commodity trading_strategy to be implemented, position sizing is a good place to begin for maximizing commodity trading profits. The generally accepted rule of thumb is for a trader not to expose more than one to three percent of the account on any given trade.

The small percentage of the account risked on each trade is typically strictly kept to in the event the trader incurs a string of losing trades. With a low percentage of an account's funding at risk per trade, a string of losers would typically not blow out the account.

While some traders use a percentage of the amount in the trading account for each trade, others prefer to build their accounts using a set dollar amount of risk per trade. Instead of one percent of the account, they will use a flat $100 per trade to build their account to the level specified in their trading plan.

One way to maximize profits with position sizing is to use a range of one to three percent of risk to be assumed on each trade. For a position that has a higher perceived probability of being profitable, the trader can make a higher percentage trade.

For example, if a special opportunity presented itself in the market that the trader had discovered through their commodity analysis, they would then make a three percent trade sized trade on that commodity. Trades which are perceived as likely to make a smaller profit would be established at the one or two percent level.

Use Trailing Stop Orders to Protect Profits

Limiting risk and maximizing profits have the common goal of preserving and increasing capital. The stop order is a good example of a trading tool used for both limiting risk and maximizing profit. Stop orders, while generally used to exit the market when the trader is wrong, are also used to protect accrued profits when used in a trailing stop strategy, for example.

A trailing stop is generally used once a profit is seen in the currency exchange rate. The stop order is then placed to ensure that a minimum profit is realized and that the underlying trend is followed to continue profiting from the move. The trailing stop order can be placed at any level worse than the market, and as the market price rises or falls, the trailing stop order is adjusted higher or lower depending on what direction the position is, but only ever towards the current market price.

When the trailing stop is eventually triggered, the trader may look for an opportunity to re-enter the market at a more favorable level or they may opt to take an opposite position if the commodity's price looks like it has reversed. Using a trailing stop loss order helps ensure that the trader's profit is not ridden into a loss, which is a classic trading error.

Consider Timed Stops in Certain Cases

Another type of stop order which is generally used as a volatility hedge is a timed stop. This type of order is not always taken by commodity brokers and is generally executed manually by the trader in a live trading account when deemed necessary. As with a regular stop order, a timed stop can be used for limiting losses or for establishing new positions.

The timed stop is a stop order with a set time limit. After a certain period of time has elapsed and the trader's order is not executed, the stop order is cancelled. When commodity prices trend, the directional push should have enough momentum to drive the price in that direction.

Nevertheless, if the anticipated market momentum does not pan out, then the move in the price can be assumed to be too weak to drive the price in the direction of the reversal or continuation pattern. After a certain amount of time passes, if the reversal to trigger the stop has not occurred, then the order is cancelled.

Maximize Profits by Understanding Trader Psychology

To be able to effectively maximize profits in commodity trading, developing a consistently profitable trading system and the discipline to adhere to its rules is the first step for a trader that wants to be a success. To develop a trading system that is profitable, a good amount of research and testing is needed, along with the proper trading psychology on the part of the trader once live trading has been initiated.

Before engaging in commodity trading in a live funded account, the best way for a trader to start is by applying their trading strategy in real market conditions in a practice or demo account, which can also be achieved the old fashion way by so-called paper trading where you just write down prospective trades in a journal. Demo trading accounts are offered by virtually every major online CFD broker, and they also usually support the Metatrader trading platform or provide a similar one of their own.

The Metatrader trading platform comes with a complete technical analysis package and software for traders to customize their own trading program. The best way to learn is by practicing, so trading in a demo account allows the trader to see weaknesses in their trading plan which can be changed before trading in a live account.

In addition, by trading in the demo account, the trader can have a firsthand experience into how well they deal with the emotions that come along with losses and profits and how well they can manage their account, all without incurring any personal financial risk.

Remember to Plan Those Trades

Traders without a proper trading plan are generally prone to panic and confusion when the market takes unexpected swings. Even with a successful trading plan, a trader can have emotional reactions which could — and generally do — adversely affect their trading.

This is the reason for taking a sufficiently long period of time to familiarize oneself with the commodity market and observe how you deal emotionally with gains and losses to ensure that consistent profits can be made once trading in a live account begins.

When it comes to optimizing trading profits, the trader's psychology is of utmost importance as a previous chapter has outlined. Avoiding getting too greedy, keeping a cool head in the face of adverse market moves, and knowing whether to pull the trigger on trades are essential elements to profitable forex trading.

Once a trader feels confident with their trading plan in a demo account, and has taken the time to know that they can be comfortable despite adverse market conditions, the trader could open a micro account, which is a margin trading account that allows trading in micro units of 0.01 and up.

A micro account can usually be opened for a nominal amount of money and gives a trader the added dimension of having a stake in their trading — albeit a small one.

The fact that the trader adheres to a specific trading plan and implements sound money management principles does wonders for a trader's overall longevity in the commodity market and can assist greatly in optimizing their commodity trading profits. This in itself is an indication that the trader has the right psychological profile to become consistently profitable.

Despite the fact that only thirty percent of trades executed via online brokers turn out to be profitable, online trading has become increasingly popular among retail commodity traders. Realistically, however, becoming a commodity trader that can show consistent profitability can generally take anywhere from six months to five years of hands on market experience.

Accordingly, do expect to spend some time getting there, and make sure to keep moving up your trader learning curve and seeking to improve your profitability results instead of stagnating at mediocre levels.

Volatility and its Effect on Trading Profits

The commodity market has been known for its volatility for a long time. Producers and industrial commodity users generally hedge many of their positions in the open market, either through forwards, futures or options.

When trading commodities, profits should be taken often and as soon as any sign of resistance to the immediate trend which led to the profit can be noted. The reason for this is that a profit in a commodity trade can turn into a loss at the drop of a dime, or more accurately after any given news or economic release that can affect the underlying supply or demand picture for the commodity. It is wise to remember that no one ever went broke by taking a profit.

Therefore, unless the trader is in a position for the long term and has considerably deep pockets, profits in commodity trading are better taken sooner than perhaps not at all. Even under these conditions if the trader has a stop loss order in at a worse rate than their entry level, that order could be hit and the trend could resume immediately afterwards.

Basically, commodity trading involves dealing with a volatility factor that could take a trader out even if they are correct in their market forecast. For this reason, many commodity traders stick to day trading or swing trading, with hedge funds, high-net-worth individual investors, financial institutions and interested corporations with deeper pockets making most of the longer term trades, which are often hedged as deemed necessary.

To maximize commodity trading profits, the key is to have consistent profits first. This entails the development of a successful trading plan with a risk management component that has been tested in a demo trading account.

Once these two elements are completed, the trader must be sufficiently disciplined to adhere to their trading plan and implement risk management successfully. After all of these conditions are met, then maximizing profits can become a priority and trailing stops can help considerably at that stage.

Trading Tips to Take Away

The following set of eight commodity trading recommendations come from the authors' own experience of trading commodities and other financial markets professionally, both for financial institutions and also for their own personal accounts.

Together, these tips form the concluding section of this commodity trading beginner's guide as you embark on your trading journey with a good solid foundation in commodity trading, market analysis and money management to build upon with your own experience. Anyway, here they are:

- **#1: Get Your Commodity Trading Started on a Good Foundation:** Reading this book was a great start for your commodity trading career since when learning to trade the commodity markets, you will first want to develop a good foundation in the mechanics of how the market works, as well as in the details of how to execute commodity transactions in your trading account and how to enter orders responsibly. Similarly, always practice trading in a demo or practice account, if possible, before using a live account to test a new online trading platform.

- **#2: Learn to Understand Market Moves:** You will also benefit greatly as a commodity trader from deepening your understanding of why the market moves. Do your homework and persistently work your way up the learning curve as your commodity knowledge base will grow from both a fundamental analysis and a technical analysis perspective.

- **#3: Consider Having a Trading Mentor:** We were both mentored by more experienced traders when we started out as professional risk takers. Most people in the early stages of their commodity trading career would benefit from finding an experienced commodity trader who can show them the ropes when it comes to trading successfully, and who can answer any questions from their seasoned and expert perspective that might arise in the beginner's mind. Remember that to get the best results from any time spent interacting with such trading mentors you should take the time in advance to prepare high-quality questions for them to answer.

- **#4: Avoid Common Commodity Trading Pitfalls:** In fine-tuning your trading process, you will also want to learn in advance what common trading pitfalls you should avoid in order to stay in business as a trader over the long term. Never fail to learn from your own mistakes or from those of others.

- **#5: Keep Emotions Out of Your Trading Decisions:** Since most trading mistakes arise from emotional involvement, remember not to emulate the trading farm animals, and vow to keep greed, fear and hope out of your trading process as much as possible.

- **#6: Develop and Test an Objective Trade Plan:** Instead of trading by the seat of your pants, take the time to develop an objective trade plan that will gradually grow your portfolio. You will also want to avoid subjecting your trading funds to excessive risk that could cause painful individual losses or longer-term draw downs.

- **#7: Plan Your Trade, and Trade Your Plan:** Your trading decisions to enter positions, take profits and cut losses should not be emotionally-based, and your trading responses should be thoroughly planned out before you pull the trigger on opening any position. Learn to follow the steps and guidelines outlined in your trade plan in a disciplined way.

- **#8: Do Not Take Risks You Cannot Afford:** Keep your optimal risk/reward ratio in mind when trading commodities and use it as a yardstick by which to measure each trade plan or individual transaction you might consider. Size your positions appropriately, protect your portfolio from excessive losses, and avoid taking any risks that might bankrupt your trading business, and never speculate with money you cannot afford to lose.

Good Luck on Your Trading Journey

If you have read this book from cover to cover, or even just skimmed it to fill in whatever gaps in your commodity trading education remained open when you first picked it up, then you should by now have an excellent foundation for moving forward more successfully and strategically as a commodity trader.

Congratulations on getting this far, and may the profitability of your commodity trading business exceed your goals and serve its desired purpose in your life.

CHAPTER 11: RECOMMENDED FURTHER READING

As an endeavor, commodity trading goes back to the age-old beginning of commerce. Fortunately, many successful traders throughout the years have written about their experiences and mistakes so that those newer to trading do not need to repeat them.

For further education on the topic of trading, the reader is first referred to the other books in this series that deal with the more advanced aspects of trading and market analysis and are written by the same professional authors.

Furthermore, most commodities exchanges and online have websites with details about each commodity contract you are interested in trading. You should review those specifications for each commodity to make sure you understand the quantities involved, the maturity date, and any delivery requirements if the contract is not cash settled.

Beyond that, a broader list of recommended commodity trading literature should probably include books on trading in general, because regardless of what market you are watching, traders of every discipline share the same overall experience.

In addition, reading books that focus solely on market analysis techniques like technical and fundamental analysis will give newer traders deeper insights into those disciplines that lay beyond the scope of this introductory book.

Classic Books on Trading in General

The first book on trading that comes to mind would have to be "Reminiscences of a Stock Operator" by Edwin Lefevre. Based on the life of Jesse Livermore, this classic book captures the attitudes and mindset of one of the most successful stock traders of the first half of the 20th century. Although the stock market was still young then, the book still gives you a good idea of what goes on in the mind of a remarkably successful trader. Although Livermore traded stocks, many of his experiences and his mindset are very relevant to commodity traders.

Two more recent bestsellers provide a useful perspective on trading for aspiring or seasoned traders alike. "The Market Wizards" and "The New Market Wizards" by Jack Schwager both contain excellent interviews with some of the world's top traders. Together, they give extraordinary insight both into the traders' psychology, as well as into how to profit in specific markets and how such top market players developed their trading systems.

Another fascinating book on trading is "The Complete Turtle Trader" by Michael Covel. The book recounts the famous story of the Turtles — a group of traders that were trained in trend-following by master trader Richard Dennis. He began this experiment as a result of a bet made with colleague William Eckhardt, and it became wildly successful. Nevertheless, some of the subjects of the experiment were not as profitable as others given the same opportunity. The book also lays out the principles and trading rules of the experiment and offers highly-educational reading for anyone serious about trading.

Further Reading on Technical Analysis and More

Although many other books are available on the subject of commodity trading, be sure that your reading on the subject includes a more detailed treatment of technical analysis. This set of techniques that use past price action to forecast the future direction of prices has become an essential subject for any trader to get a grasp of, no matter whether they wish to trade in the stock, forex or commodities markets.

Most seasoned technical analysts would agree that the bible of technical analysis is "Technical Analysis of the Financial Markets: A Comprehensive Guide to Trading Methods and Applications" by John G. Murphy. This book gives a complete overview of all major market and is an invaluable resource for both new and professional traders.

Many other fine books on trading can be found, and the New York Institute of Finance publishes an especially good collection of books on markets and trading. Remember, the more you know about the subject of trading and the market you have chosen to participate in, the more prepared you will be when you make decisions as a trader.

Basically, when it comes to trading, knowledge really is power, and knowing how to apply that knowledge generally distinguishes successful traders from the rest of the pack.

ABOUT THE AUTHORS

Jay and Julie Hawk are a husband and wife team who currently trade commodities, currencies and financial products online for their own account and have worked in the financial markets in several different occupations. Together, they have more than 40 years of professional experience trading in the financial markets.

For her part, Julie completed her scientific research degree and started out working as a business systems analyst for a major investment bank where she became qualified as a Series 7 Registered Representative and was thoroughly trained in all major financial products. She also attended the well-known O'Connell and Piper options training course in Chicago. She later worked as a dealer in the trading rooms of several major international banks in New York City, London and San Francisco, eventually working her way up to the vice president level.

In that capacity, Julie was personally involved in educating, providing customized hedging and risk taking strategies, meeting with other corporate executives, and handling large scale transactions for high-profile banking clients including large corporations, fund managers and high net worth individuals. She also traded substantial options portfolios for her employers as a risk manager, including exotic options like binary, barrier, average rate and basket options. She even received a notable award for her creativity, teamwork and profitability in executing unusual and highly profitable derivatives transactions.

During that time, Julie also developed world-class expertise in technical analysis, including Elliott Wave Theory, and was involved in initiating research into automated trading and trading signal systems. She also joined the San Francisco Writers' Guild and regularly wrote trade strategies, educational material, market commentary, market newsletters, reports, articles and press releases. In addition, Julie was interviewed for various financial markets magazines and for news wires such as REUTERS in her professional capacity as a financial markets expert.

In contrast to Julie's highly professional and elite banking role, Jay's professional trading experience was focused more on futures and options exchange floor trading activities, fund management, and fundamental research-based commodity trading and stock investing. After growing up in Chicago and then moving to Mexico City, Jay returned to Chicago to begin working in the futures and options markets on the Chicago Board Options Exchange just a few years after the exchange was founded.

In addition to working his way up to holding a seat and operating as a market maker on several options exchanges in Chicago and San Francisco, Jay also ran a retail stock brokerage desk and managed funds for a number of large institutional investors that he traded profitably on a discretionary basis and that included commodity trades. Jay later took a position on the Chicago Mercantile Exchange where he helped start up and actively traded in listed commodity futures and options. He eventually moved to the West Coast to start trading on the Pacific Options Exchange, where he focused largely on trading stock options and the underlying stocks.

After both independently retiring from their professional trading careers as relatively wealthy people, Jay and Julie met up, fell love and got married to raise a child together just after the new millennium dawned. They moved to Mexico to semi-retire near the beach and operate an Internet-based business together, but they soon discovered that the financial and commodity markets had become more accessible to retail traders via online brokers and the availability of CFDs. This incredible opportunity seemed too tempting for these seasoned traders to ignore!

They also observed a demand for educational material to be provided to retail traders via the Internet, and that the quality of existing written content available online was rather poor. That led them to start a new career together as freelance writers specializing in writing about the financial and commodity markets using their professional background and expertise. This eventually resulted in them co-founding TheFXperts (located online at www.thefxperts.com) to provide clients with expertly-written market content, trader mentoring and financial consulting.

Jay and Julie are very pleased to present this book as the third in a series of books on trading that they will be releasing over the coming years. You can visit TheFXperts' website to learn about their future book releases.

GLOSSARY

Aluminum: Refers to a bluish silver-white malleable and ductile light metal with good electrical and thermal conductivity, as well as high reflectivity and resistance to oxidation. Aluminum is the most abundant minor metal in the earth's crust and generally occurs in combination with other elements. Standard aluminum futures contracts are traded on the London Metals Exchange and are quoted in U.S. dollars.

Capital Markets: A global marketplace where all financial instruments like commodities, currencies, stocks and bonds are traded.

Closing Price: The final closing amount of money at which a commodity or other asset has traded at on a given trading day. In markets that trade round the clock, the closing price is determined at a certain hour of the day for the region in which the asset is traded. For example, the CME closes commodity futures trading each weekday at 5:00pm EST and then re-opens for electronic trading at 6pm EST.

Coffee: Refers to the seeds of berries of the Coffea plant, a native of tropical Africa. Coffee is a top agricultural commodity export for a number of countries and the most traded agricultural commodity in the world, as well as one of the most valuable commodities of developing nations. Coffee futures are traded on the NYMEX or New York Mercantile Exchange under the symbol KC and are quoted in USD dollars per pound. Each futures contract is for 37,500 pounds.

Copper: Refers to a soft, malleable native metal with high electrical and thermal conductivity. Copper is used as material for wire and other building materials, as well as a constituent of alloys, in coins and jewelry. Copper futures are traded on the COMEX division of the NYMEX under the symbol HG and are quoted in USD cents per pound. Each futures contract is for 25,000 pounds.

Cotton: Refers to a soft staple cellulose fiber derived from the boll around the seeds of the cotton plant of the genus Gossypium. Cotton is used in the production of fabrics such as denim, corduroy, chino and terrycloth. Cotton futures trade on the New York Board of Trade under the symbol CT. Price fluctuations are in cents and hundredths of a USD cent per pound. Each futures contract is for 50,000 pounds.

Crude Oil: Also known as petroleum is a black, brown or yellow liquid that naturally occurs in geological formations beneath the Earth's surface. Crude oil is refined into a number of fuels that include gasoline, jet fuel, diesel, as well as lubricating oil. Light Sweet Crude Oil futures are traded on the New York Mercantile Exchange under the symbol CL. Price fluctuations are shown in USD cents per barrel with a contract size of 1,000 U.S. barrels or 42,000 gallons of crude oil.

Dealing Spread: The difference or spread between the immediate prices at which a dealer, broker or market maker is willing to buy and sell a particular commodity or other asset. The dealing spread is composed of a low bid price and a higher offer price which respectively represent where a market maker is willing to buy and sell the asset.

Ethanol: Also known as alcohol, drinking alcohol or ethyl alcohol, is a colorless liquid that is naturally produced by the process of fermentation of sugars by yeast or through a petrochemical process. Ethanol is produced in the manufacture of alcoholic beverages and used as an antiseptic, disinfectant and chemical solvent, as well as a source of clean burning fuel. Ethanol futures are traded at the Chicago Board of Trade and are quoted in USD dollars and cents. Each ethanol futures contract is for 29,000 gallons of ethanol.

Flight to Quality: the tendency of investors to seek the safest possible assets for their money during challenging economic times. By doing so, they generally move their funds out of riskier, low-quality assets and into more conservative, higher-quality assets like precious metals that are generally perceived as safer investments.

Fundamental Analysis: A method of research that involves determining a commodity or other asset's intrinsic value by investigating the related financial and economic factors that influence its valuation. These factors could be related to the supply, demand, production and company's management, macro or microeconomic data and would determine if the security or asset is fairly valued, undervalued or overvalued.

Futures Contract: A standardized and transferable agreement traded on an exchange the price of which depends on that of an underlying asset. The delivery dates for such futures contracts will generally fall on a particular set of dates, often quarterly, in order to provide greater liquidity. Futures trade in amounts that are multiples of the standard lot size for the contract.

Futures Market: Refers to a system for trading futures contracts, which are agreements to transact a certain amount of a commodity on a future date. Futures markets consist of centralized exchanges located in various countries that are part of the overall commodities market.

Gold: Refers to a precious metal that is bright and yellow, ductile and malleable and occurs naturally in alluvial deposits, in rocks, veins and as grains or in the form of nuggets. Gold is a traditional store of wealth and is widely used in the jewelry business, in electronics and in the medical field. Gold futures are traded on the COMEX division of the New York Mercantile Exchange and are quoted in USD dollars and cents per troy ounce. The gold futures contract is for 100 Troy ounces.

Heating Oil: Refers to a liquid derivative of petroleum used primarily as a fuel for boilers and furnaces in buildings. Heating Oil futures are traded on the New York Mercantile Exchange under the symbol HO and quoted in USD dollars and cents per gallon. Heating Oil futures contracts are for 42,000 U.S. gallons or 1,000 barrels.

Lead: Refers to a malleable poor, non-ferrous metal considered to be one of the "heavy metals" and used primarily for bullets, solder, lead-acid batteries and radiation shields. Standard lead futures contracts on lead of 99.97% purity are traded on the London Metals Exchange and are quoted in U.S. dollars.

Lean Hogs: Refers to industrially raised Hogs used for pork meat and is the main source of pork meat sold in the United States. Lean Hog futures trade on the Chicago Mercantile Exchange and on the CME electronic Globex trading platform.

Leverage: In finance, leverage is the use of debt for the financing of an activity. For example, an individual paying for a property with a mortgage or a company that has more than 80 percent debt relative to its assets would be considered leveraged. In commodities trading, leverage is achieved by using margin, which calls for a fraction of funds to be deposited in a margin account in order to control the purchase or short sale of securities.

Light Sweet Crude Oil: Refers to a type of petroleum which contains less than 0.5% sulfur giving it the "sweet" versus "sour" petroleum with a higher sulfuric content. Light Sweet Crude Oil is primarily refined into gasoline, diesel fuel and kerosene. Light Sweet Crude Oil futures trade on the New York Mercantile Exchange, as well as on the CME Globex and ClearPort electronic trading platforms.

Linear Low Density Polyethylene or LLDPE: Refers to a linear polymer or polyethylene with short branches made by copolymerization of ethylene; the process produces a polymer with a linear structure and a narrower molecular weight distribution than regular low density polyethylene. LLDPE is widely used to manufacture a wide range of plastic products from plastic bags to toys and flexible tubing. Linear Low Density Polyethylene futures contracts trade on the London Metals Exchange and are deliverable in North America, Asia and Europe. LLDPE contracts also trade on the Dalian Commodity Exchange in Dalian, China, where contracts are quoted in Chinese renminbi.

Live Cattle: Refers to cattle industrially raised for beef production which is from the calf stage until they reach between 600 to 800 pounds at which point they are considered Feeder Cattle and taken to feedlots to continue the fattening process. The Feeder Cattle eventually reach 1,250 pounds at which point they are slaughtered. Live Cattle futures trade on the Chicago Mercantile Exchange and on the CME Globex platform.

Livestock: Refers to animals that are raised for meat products such as hogs and cattle. Livestock also includes oxen, horses, sheep, goats, pigs, buffalo, mules and donkeys. As part of an agricultural system, raising livestock is an expensive endeavor requiring time and energy, and hence results in high meat prices. Livestock futures on Lean Hogs, Feeder and Live Cattle and Frozen Pork Bellies are traded on the Chicago Mercantile Exchange and on the CME electronic Globex trading platform.

LMEmini: Refers to mini-contracts offered by the London Metals Exchange for Grade A Copper, Zinc of 99.995% minimum purity and Aluminum of 99.7% minimum purity. The contracts are half the size of normal LME metals contracts and are for five tonnes per contract. LMEmini contracts are quoted in U.S. Dollars. Contracts are for cash settlement meaning no physical delivery is available, and they are traded electronically through the LME Select system and on the telephone market.

LMEX: Refers to the London Metals Exchange Metals Index. A weighted index of six designated primary metals, which include: Primary Aluminum, Zinc, Nickel, Lead, Copper and Tin. The Index has both futures and options and are quoted in U.S. Dollars, the Index is traded in Index points with each Index point valued at $10.00 USD. Futures contracts trade in all months and are for cash settlement of the difference between the Index on the prompt date and the value of the Index in the contract multiplied by contract size.

Margin: A collateral amount used in the purchase or sale of futures contracts or CFDs. The margin for a purchase consists of the collateral amount that the buyer of the instrument needs to put up with the broker to cover the amount of risk of the transaction. For example, for the purchase of Heating Oil futures contracts worth $100,000, a margin deposit of 20 percent of the total notional amount or $20,000 is required by the broker or exchange to make the purchase.

Market Close: The end of a trading session for any particular market. For example, the market close of the Chicago Mercantile Exchange occurs each weekday at 5:00PM Eastern Standard Time. A closed market refers to exchange holidays when no trading takes place.

Market Maker: An individual who makes two way prices on certain commodities, usually to clients or on exchanges. They may also watch and execute orders for clients.

Mentha Oil: Refers to the oil from the Mint or Mentha plant genus, which consists of 25 perennial herbs of the Lamiaceae family. Mentha Oil is commonly used as a flavoring in breath fresheners, toothpaste, chewing gum and other products. The oil is also used in medicine, cosmetics, and insecticides, as well as an additive to cigarettes. Mentha Oil futures trade on three commodities exchanges in India: the Multi Commodity Exchange of India (MCX), the National Commodities and Derivatives Exchange (NCDEX), and the National Multi-Commodity Exchange. Each exchange has its own quality and contract specifications and contracts are generally quoted in Indian Rupees.

Mild Steel Ingot: Refers to ingots of "mild steel," which is a semi-finished class of steel with a low amount of carbon, typically from 0.01 to 0.3% used to make long steel products. This commodity is used mainly in the construction industry and for roads, bridges and other such infrastructure. Mild Steel Ingot futures are traded on the Multi Commodity Exchange of India (MCX) and the National Commodities & Derivatives Exchange (NCDEX) also in India.

Milk Class III: Refers to all Grade A and Grade B milk which is used in the manufacture of other products other than that prescribed for Milk Class I, fluid milk marketed as such, and Milk Class II, which is used for cottage cheese and yogurt. Milk Class III is generally used for the production of cheese. Milk Class III futures contracts are traded on the Chicago Mercantile Exchange and on the CME electronic Globex trading platform.

Milk Class IV: Refers to all Grade A and Grade B milk which is used in the manufacture of products other than that prescribed for Milk Class I, fluid milk marketed as such, and Milk Class II, which is used for cottage cheese and yogurt, and Milk Class III, which is used for the production of cheese. Milk Class IV is used to produce butter and non-fat dry milk. Milk Class IV futures contracts are traded at the Chicago Mercantile Exchange and on the CME electronic Globex trading platform.

Mini Sized Corn: Refers to mini-sized corn futures contracts traded on the CME. Corn is a tall cereal grass which grows kernels on ears and is used for food for humans and animals. Corn grows throughout the world and has been the predominant cereal for centuries in Mexico and Central America.

Mini Sized Soybeans: Refers to Mini-Sized Soybean futures contracts traded on the CME. Soybeans are an oilseed legume originally from East Asia that has been used for centuries as a protein source both for humans and animals. Soybeans are also used to make oil and meal.

Mini Sized Wheat: Refers to Mini-Sized Soybean futures contracts traded on the CME. Wheat is a grain grass which originated in the Fertile Crescent area of the Near East, and is now cultivated worldwide. Wheat grain is a world staple food used in the making of flour for bread, breakfast cereal, noodles, beer and other alcoholic products as well as biofuel.

Minor Metals: Refers to metals that are insufficiently active or are not of wide enough interest to be listed on the London Metals Exchange or other large commodity exchange for trading, although the LME recently launched futures on the minor metals Molybdenum and Cobalt. Other minor metals include: Antimony, Bismuth, Ferro-Chrome, Germanium, Manganese, Mercury, Indium, Selenium, Silicon and Tungsten.

miNY Gold: Refers to mini-sized gold futures contracts traded electronically on the Chicago Mercantile Exchange's Globex electronic trading platform. Gold is a precious metal used for wealth storage and as an inflation hedge.

miNY Silver: Refers to to mini-sized silver futures contracts traded electronically on the Chicago Mercantile Exchange's Globex electronic trading platform. Silver is a precious metal used for wealth storage, as an inflation hedge and for a number of other industrial uses.

Molybdenum: A minor metal with a silvery appearance used primarily in high-strength steel alloys because of having the sixth-highest melting point of any element, Molybdenum is also used in high-temperature and high-pressure applications such as catalysts and pigments. Molybdenum futures trade on the London Metals Exchange or LME.

NASAAC: An acronym for the North American Special Aluminum Alloy Contract. These futures contracts are traded on the London Metals Exchange or LME.

Natural Gas: A gaseous mixture of hydrocarbons that occurs naturally in porous rock below the earth's surface. The mixture of gases consists of methane, ethane, and in smaller levels, propane and butane. Natural Gas is widely used for cooking and heating homes as well as other uses. Natural Gas futures are traded on the New York Mercantile Exchange and on the Chicago Mercantile Exchange's Globex and ClearPort electronic trading platforms.

New York Harbor Ultra Low Sulfur Diesel: A diesel fuel futures contract traded on the New York Mercantile Exchange or NYMEX. Ultra Low Sulfur Diesel is a new standard for highway diesel fuel in the United States that took effect across the nation as of December, 2010.

Nickel: A silvery lustrous metal that is corrosion resistant and used in alloys, in the manufacture of coins, magnets and other products. The American Nickel coin is made of 75% copper and 25% Nickel. Nickel futures contracts trade on the London Metals Exchange LME and are for Nickel of 99.8% purity.

Non Ferrous Metals: Refers to non-magnetic metals that do not contain iron. Such metals are used in manufacturing appliances, furniture, electronic equipment, packaging and aluminum foil. Futures on Non-Ferrous Metals trade on a number of exchanges, with the London Metals Exchange LME being the principle market. The LME currently trades contracts on non-ferrous metals including: Aluminum, Aluminum Alloy, Copper, Lead, Tin, Nickel and Zinc.

Nonfat Dry Milk Spot Call: Refers to nonfat dry milk contracts that are traded for same-day delivery by open outcry on the floor of the Chicago Mercantile Exchange. Nonfat Dry Milk is a powdery substance obtained from milk.

Nonfat Dry Milk: Generally refers to Deliverable Nonfat Dry Milk which is a dairy product derived from whole milk. This dairy product is traded as a futures contract on the GLOBEX and ClearPort electronic trading platforms of the Chicago Mercantile Exchange.

NYMEX Softs: Refers to agricultural commodities futures such as Cocoa, Coffee, Cotton and No. 11 Sugar that are traded on the New York Mercantile Exchange or NYMEX. Softs are traded both on the NYMEX floor and on the Chicago Mercantile Exchange's Globex electronic trading platform. The NYMEX Softs commodities futures all have their own specifications of size and settlement and are all quoted in U.S. Dollars with varying minimum fluctuations.

Oats: A type of cereal grain known as *Avena sativa* which is grown for its seed generally in temperate climates. Oats are consumed by humans in the form of oatmeal and rolled oats; however, they are primarily used as a feed for livestock. Oat futures are traded on the CME.

Oil Seeds: Refers to all class of seeds from which oil is derived. Many oil seeds are industrially grown to produce oil for human consumption. Seeds which are grown and traded as commodities include: soya, cottonseed, corn, rapeseed, olive, sesame and sunflower seeds among others. After the extraction process, the oil residue can be used as a source of protein for animal feed such as oil-seed cake and presscake.

Over-the-Counter or OTC: Refers to a decentralized market in which assets or financial instruments are not traded on an official exchange. In general, such OTC instruments will instead be dealt directly between counterparties over the telephone or via some other reliable means of communicating contractual terms, like an electronic dealing system for example.

Palladium: A soft, tarnish resistant and silvery metallic element that occurs naturally in a variety of ores such as those of platinum, gold and copper. Palladium is considered a precious and an industrial metal with a wide array of uses, such as in the manufacture of catalytic converters for the automotive industry. Palladium futures trade on the New York Mercantile Exchange and the CME Globex and ClearPort electronic trading platforms.

Plastics Futures: Refers to futures on plastics products such as Polypropylene and Linear Low Density Polyethylene. Futures contracts on both products are traded on the London Metals Exchange or LME.

LLDPE contracts also trade on the Dalian Commodity Exchange in Dalian, China where contracts are quoted in Chinese renminbi.

Platinum: A precious metal primarily used in the production of jewelry, as well as in chemical and petroleum refining and in the manufacture of automotive catalyst systems. Roughly 80% of the world's platinum supply originates in South Africa, with 10% coming from Russia and the rest from North America. Platinum futures are traded on the New York Mercantile Exchange and the Chicago Mercantile Exchange's Globex and ClearPort electronic trading platforms.

Polypropylene: A light, rigid thermoplastic material derived from the polymerization of propylene. Polypropylene is used in a wide range of industrial applications such as the production of fabrics, carpets and upholstery as well as in the manufacture of plastic containers for foods, cosmetics and other liquids. Polypropylene futures contracts trade on the London Metals Exchange and are quoted in U.S. Dollars per ton.

Polyvinyl Chloride or PVC: A polymer of vinyl chloride made into a vinyl resin with a wide array of industrial uses. Polyvinyl chloride is used in making wrapping plastic for food as well as more rigid items such as pipes, upholstery and fibers. Polyvinyl Chloride futures trade on the National Commodities Exchange of India, as well as on the Mumbai Multi-Commodities Exchange and the Dalian Commodities Exchange of China.

Precious Metals: Metallic substances that have a high intrinsic economic value. Such metals are rare and serve as a store of intrinsic wealth for nations and individuals, as well as having various industrial applications. Precious metals include: gold, silver, palladium and platinum. They are traded on many of the world's largest commodity exchanges, such as the New York Mercantile Exchange, the London Metals Exchange and the Chicago Mercantile Exchange.

Random Length Lumber: Refers to boards of wood of varying lengths, usually in two-foot increments. The variety of different lengths can vary greatly between different tree species and manufacturers. Lumber futures are traded on the Chicago Mercantile Exchange under the symbol LB and are quoted in USD dollars per 1,000 board feet. Each Random Length Lumber futures contract is for 110,000 board feet of lumber.

Range: A set of market prices bounded on the top by the high price and on the bottom by the low price of a futures contract or other asset observed during a particular trading time frame. For example, if WTI Crude

Oil had a daily high of $60 per barrel and a daily low of $55 per barrel, then the range of that contract during the trading day was $55-$60.

Raw Jute: Refers to a natural fiber derived from a plant known as Corchorus. Jute is the second cheapest natural fiber after cotton and is collected from the skin of the plant. Jute futures are traded on the Indian National Commodity and Derivatives Exchange Ltd. and the National Multi Commodity Exchange of India Ltd. or NCDEX and NMCE respectively.

RBD Palm Olein: Refers to a derivative of a palm species known as E. Guineesis, which grows in Southeast Asia. Unlike palm oil, which is derived from the same plant, Palm Olein is highly heat resistant and remains in a liquid form at room temperature. RBD stands for "refined, bleached and deodorized". Palm Olein futures trade on the Bursa Malaysia Derivatives Exchange under the symbol FPOL and is quoted in USD dollars per ton. Each RBD Palm Olein futures contract represents 25 metric tons of Palm Olein.

Refined Soya Oil: Refers to an oil extracted from soybean seeds — Glycine max — which is then subjected to refining using a process of water degumming and chemical and physical refining. Refined Soya Oil is one of the most widely used oils in cooking. Soya Oil Futures trade on the Chicago Board of Trade and are quoted in USD cents and hundredths of cents per pound. The Soya Oil futures contract is for 60,000 pounds per contract.

Resistance: A technical term that refers to an excess of supply of a commodity at a given price level. For example, if a commodity futures contract trades up to $12 per lot after opening at $10, and then trades back to $10, then the resistance level for that particular time frame would be at the $12 price the market reversed at.

Rough Rice: Refers to unmilled whole rice grain that comes directly from the field after being harvested. Rough Rice is also known as whole grain rice, paddy rice and hulled rice. Rough Rice futures contracts trade on the CME Group's Globex Exchange and are quoted in USD cents per hundredweight. The Rough Rice futures contract is for 2,000 hundredweights or 91 metric tons.

Rubber: Also known as India rubber or caoutchouc, a naturally occurring substance harvested in the form of latex from the rubber tree or *Hevea brasiliensis*. Rubber is mainly produced in Southeast Asia and is a widely used commodity in the manufacture of automobile tires, hoses, gaskets and many other products. Natural Rubber futures are traded on the Shanghai Futures Exchange or SHFE and quoted in Renminbi per ton. Each futures contract is for 10 tons of Natural Rubber.

Silver: A white lustrous precious metal with the highest thermal and electrical conductivity and the highest reflectivity of any metal. The metal is naturally occurring and found in the Earth's crust. In addition to its use in coins and as a store of wealth, silver is used extensively in jewelry, water filtration, medicine and solar panels. Silver futures trade on the CME's Globex and ClearPort exchanges under the SI symbol and are quoted in USD dollars and cents. The contract unit is for 5,000 troy ounces of silver.

Soya Bean: Refers to Glycine max, a species of legume originating in East Asia that is widely cultivated for its edible bean and has a number of derivatives such as oil, soybean meal and soybean crush, what is known in the commodity world as the soybean complex. Soybean futures trade on the CME's Globex Exchange under the symbol ZS and on the ClearPort Exchange under the S symbol. The Soybean futures contract is for 5,000 bushels and is quoted in ¼ of one USD cent ($12.50) per bushel.

Soybean Crush: A type of commodity spread that involves the trader going long soybean futures while shorting soybean meal and soybean oil futures, thereby establishing a processing margin. Soybeans are converted into two products, meal and oil, which is achieved through "crushing". The Crush Spread is a gauge of the soybean processor's profit margin obtained from processing soybeans. The Crush Spread is traded on the Chicago Board of Trade under the symbol BCX are quoted in USD dollars and cents and consists of buying one Soybean contract and selling one Soybean Oil contract and one Soybean Meal contract.

Soybean Meal: Refers to a soybean derivative that is widely used in animal feeds and as a protein supplement. Approximately 98 percent of soybean meal production is used as animal feed, with the remaining two percent used in other food products for human consumption. Soybean Meal futures trade on CME Group's Globex Exchange under the symbol ZM and are quoted in USD dollars and cents per ton. The Soybean Meal futures contract is for 100 short tons of meal.

Steel: A high tensile strength alloy composed of carbon, iron and other components. Steel is a metal product that is durable and low in cost. The alloy is used in the construction of buildings, automobiles, machinery, weapons and appliances to name only a few. Steel futures trade on the CME ClearPort Exchange under the symbol FSF and are quoted in USD 0.01 per metric ton. The Steel Futures contract is for 50 metric tons of steel.

Sugar: A derivative product of the sugar cane and sugar beet plants. With more than 160 million metric tons of sugar produced every year, sugar is one of the most subsidized crops in the world. Due to its use in ethanol production and higher oil prices, sugar prices have risen over the last two years. Sugar No. 11 futures contract is traded on the ICE futures exchange and is quoted in USD cents and hundredths of a cent per pound. The Sugar No. 11 futures contract is for 112,000 pounds of raw sugar.

Support: A technical analysis term that refers to an abundance of buy orders at a certain price level in a commodity or other asset. When its price reaches a level of support, the asset tends to move higher until reaching a level, known as resistance, where an excess of supply puts downward pressure on its price.

Technical Analysis: A method of investigation into the price patterns of commodities or other assets that depends on the levels of supply and demand. Technical analysis indicates at what prices assets are most likely to appreciate or decline by using indicators such as oscillators, moving averages and volume figures.

Tin: Refers to a non-ferrous base metal used mostly in the electronics industry as solder. Tin is also used as a plating element and as a major ingredient in the production of bronze. Tin futures trade on the London Metals Exchange or LME under the symbol SN and are quoted in USD dollars per tonne. The Tin futures contract is for 5 tonnes.

Trend: The prevailing direction of asset prices. For example, an upward trend would indicate that the price of a commodity is gaining, while a downward trend would indicate that its price is falling. Three major trends types can be discerned in an asset market: rising, declining and flat.

Wheat: Refers to a grass — Triticum — cultivated for its seed, which produces a cereal grain used widely in the production of many food products. Wheat futures are traded under the symbol W on the Chicago Board of Trade and are quoted in USD ¼ cent per bushel. The Wheat futures contract is for 5,000 bushels.

Wood Pulp: Refers to a lignocellulosic fibrous substance produced by mechanically or chemically separating cellulose fiber from wood. Wood Pulp is the main source for paper. Wood Pulp futures are traded on the CME's Globex Exchange under the symbol WP and quoted in USD $0.50 per metric ton. The Wood Pulp futures contract is for 20 metric tons.

Yellow Peas: Refers to a legume widely cultivated in North America, Asia, Europe and parts of the Middle East. Yellow Pea futures are traded under the symbol YPEASKPR on the National Commodity and Derivatives Exchange in India. The minimum fluctuation is of 1 Rupee per ton and the contract size is for 10 metric tons.

Zinc: Refers to a chemical element similar to magnesium and a transition metal. Zinc is the fourth most common metal and is most often used for galvanizing and for batteries. Zinc futures trade on the CME Globex and ClearPort Exchanges under the symbol ZNC. The contract is quoted in USD dollars and cents per metric ton and is for 25 metric tons per contract.

INDEX

Aluminum, 189
Analysis Paralysis, 142
Anger, 151
Animal Farm, 147
Automated Trading, 97
Automated Trading Software, 114
Automated Trading Systems, 56
Automatic Trading, 56
Averaging, 136
Base Metals, 61
Bears, 148
Bid and Offer, 47
Bid/offer, 92, 94, 138
Broker, 38, 41
Bulls, 147, 153
Business Plan, 161
Business Risk, 167, 168
Capital Markets, 189
Cash-Settled Futures, 31
CFD broker, 98
Chart Patterns, 102, 108, 110

Charting Service, 105
Chicago Mercantile Exchange, 5
Chickens, 149
Clearing Trades, 30
Closing Price, 189
CME Group, 5
Coffee, 78, 189
Commercial Need, 40
Commitment of Traders, 122
Commodity, 1
Commodity Exchanges, 23
Commodity Valuation, 126
Commodity Trading, 23
Consolidation Patterns, 110
Consumer Price Index, 121
Continuation Patterns, 110
Copper, 69, 189
Cotton, 80, 190
Crude Oil, 71, 190
Currencies, 120
Dalian Commodities Exchange, 6
Day Traders, 86

Day Trading, 85
Dealing Prices, 46
Dealing Spread, 92, 190
Delivery, 30, 52
Demo Testing, 162
Depression, 151
Directional Movement Indicator, 107
Discipline, 89, 142, 156, 163
Double Top or Bottom, 112
Economic Data, 121
Economic Risk, 168
Edwin Lefevre, 182
Electronic Trading, 25, 97
Emotional Responses, 165
Emotions, 146, 150, 152, 154, 165, 166, 178
Employment Data, 121
Energy, 3, 71
Ethanol, 75, 190
Exchange Floor, 28
Exchanges, 1
Excitement, 151
Exercising, 36
Fear, 146, 150, 151, 152
Flags, 111
Flight to Quality, 190
Floor Brokers, 29
Forward Contracts, 6
Fundamental Analysis, 117, 190
Fundamental Data, 121
Fundamental Risks, 139
Fundamentals, 38, 125, 127
Further Reading, 181
Futures, 6
Futures Contract, 191
Futures Market, 191
Geopolitical events, 122
Gold, 62, 191
Greed, 133, 137, 139, 146, 147, 149, 151, 153, 156, 164
Gross Domestic Product, 121
Head and Shoulders, 112

Heating Oil, 73, 191
Hedging, 15, 16
Hope, 146, 151, 153
Human Behavior, 117
Illiquidity, 137
Industrial Production, 121
Investment, 40
Jack Schwager, 182
John G. Murphy, 182
John Murphy, 104
Last Trading Day, 32
Last Trading Days, 53
Lead, 191
Lean Hogs, 191
leverage, 132
Leverage, 191
Light Sweet Crude Oil, 192
Limit Orders, 49
Linear Low Density Polyethylene, 192
Live Cattle, 192
Livestock, 192
LLDPE, 192
LMEmini, 192
LMEX, 193
Locals, 29
London Metals Exchange, 5
Managing Emotions, 154
Margin, 193
Margin Calls, 89, 155, 168
Market Close, 193
Market Orders, 49
Market Participants, 13
Market-Makers, 92
Market-Making, 92
Mentha Oil, 193
Metals, 3
MetaTrader, 97, 98, 105, 114, 175
Michael Covel, 182
Mild Steel Ingot, 193
Milk Class III, 194
Milk Class IV, 194
Mindset, 155, 156, 159

Mini Sized Corn, 194
Mini Sized Soybeans, 194
Mini Sized Wheat, 194
Minor Metals, 194
miNY Gold, 194
miNY Silver, 194
Molybdenum, 195
Money Management, 60, 131, 133, 135, 162
Moving Averages, 94, 106, 109
Multi-Commodity Exchange, 6
NASAAC, 195
National Multi-Commodity and Derivatives Exchange, 6
Natural Gas, 195
NCDEX. *See* National Multi-Commodity and Derivatives Exchange
New York Harbor Ultra Low Sulfur Diesel, 195
News, 116, 129
Nickel, 195
Non Ferrous Metals, 195
Nonfat Dry Milk, 196
Nonfat Dry Milk Spot Call, 195
Non-Transferable Notices, 31
Notice Days, 32
NYMEX Softs, 196
Oats, 196
OCO Order. *See* One-Cancels-the-Other Order
Oil Seeds, 196
One-Cancels-the-Other Order, 50
Online Broker, 38, 49
Online CFD broker, 98
Online Trading, 14
Optimizing profits, 172
Options, 34
OTC. *See* Over-the-Counter
Over leveraging, 136
Over-the-Counter, 1, 24, 32, 196
Overtrading, 142, 153

Palladium, 67, 196
Pattern-Matching, 113
Pennants, 111
Physical Commodities, 9
Pigs, 149
Plastics, 196
Platinum, 66, 197
Political Events, 124
Polypropylene, 197
Polyvinyl Chloride, 197
Position Sizing, 133, 158, 173
Precious Metals, 197
Price Analysis, 101
Price Quotes, 47
Prices, 45
Probability of Success, 59
Producer Price Index, 121
Psychology, 145, 146, 154, 155, 162
PVC, 197
Random Length Lumber, 197
Range, 197
Range Traders, 88
Raw Jute, 198
RBD Palm Olein, 198
Rectangles, 111
Refined Soya Oil, 198
Relative Strength Index, 91, 103, 107, 109
Resistance, 103, 109, 198
Retail Sales, 121
Reversal Patterns, 111
Risk Management, 134, 164, 172
Risks, 137, 153, 167, 168, 178
Rough Rice, 198
RSI. *See* Relative Strength Index
Rubber, 198
Scalper, 93
Scalping, 92
Sheep, 149
Silver, 64, 199
Soft Commodities, 77
Soya Bean, 199

Soybean Complex, 96
Soybean Crush, 199
Soybean Meal, 199
Specialist, 193
Speculation, 8, 16, 40
Spot Market, 6
Spread Trading, 94
Steel, 199
Stop Orders, 50
Stop-loss, 132
Stop-loss Orders, 134, 136
Sugar, 81, 200
Supply and Demand, 10, 119, 122
Support, 103, 109, 200
Swing Trading, 89, 90, 91
Taking Profits, 153
Tax Code, 168
Technical Analysis, 39, 102, 103, 104, 112, 113, 115, 127, 182, 200
Technical Analysis Software, 112, 113, 114, 115
Technical Indicators, 103, 106, 107, 109
Technical Newsletter, 104
TheFXperts, 186
Timed Stops, 174
Tin, 200
Trade Balance, 121
Trade Journal, 157
Trade Plan, 105, 106, 163, 164, 165, 166, 178
Trade Signal Generating Software, 114
Trader Psychology, 145, 174
Trading, 133
Trading Commodities, 8

Trading Decisions, 178
Trading Errors, 138
Trading Goals, 162
Trading Mechanics, 37
Trading Mentor, 178
Trading Pitfalls, 178
Trading Plan, 39, 59, 86, 89, 106, 110, 131, 135, 138, 139, 145, 153, 154, 156, 157, 158, 159, 162, 163, 164, 167
Trading Platforms, 53
Trading Psychology, 162
Trading Risks, 137, 141, 142
Trading Robot, 98, 106, 114
Trading Signal Generators, 57
Trading Signals, 108
Trading Software, 96
Trading Strategies, 85
Trading Tips, 58, 177
Trailing Stop Orders, 173
Trailing Stops, 134
Transferable Notices, 31
Trend, 200
Trend Traders, 87
Trend Trading, 87, 91
Triangles, 110, 111, 112
Triple Top or Bottom, 112
Volatility, 137, 176
Volume Indicators, 107
Weather, 119, 122, 140
Wedges, 111
West Texas Intermediate, 72
Wheat, 200
Wood Pulp, 201
Yellow Peas, 201
Zinc, 201

www.ingramcontent.com/pod-product-compliance
Lightning Source LLC
Chambersburg PA
CBHW020644220526
45464CB00001B/283